MUSIC ACTIVITIES FOR SPECIAL CHILDREN

Ruth Zinar, Ph.D.

Parker Publishing Company, Inc.
West Nyack, New York

© 1987 *by*

PARKER PUBLISHING COMPANY, INC.
West Nyack, New York

Library of Congress Cataloging-in-Publication Data

Zinar, Ruth, 1920–
  Music activities for special children.

  Bibliography: p.
  Includes index.
    1. Exceptional children—Education—Music.
  2. Handicapped children—Education—Music.
  3. School music—Instruction and study.   I. Title.
MT17.Z56   1987   371.9'044   86-30308

ISBN 0-13-606922-3

Printed in the United States of America

To *Milton*

About the Author

Ruth Zinar is a Professor of Music Education at York College of the City University of New York, and has taught music at all levels from early childhood classes through college. She has a master's degree in music and music education from Columbia University and a Ph.D. in Music Education from New York University. She has written numerous articles on music education and musicology, and has given music lectures and workshops for many teachers' groups. Her contributions to music education have been internationally recognized by citations in *Leaders in Education* and *International Who's Who in Music.*

Dr. Zinar is also the author of *Music in Your Classroom: An Activities Program for Music Skills, Appreciation, and Creativity* (Parker Publishing Company, Inc., 1983).

About This Book

Music offers every child an opportunity for fun, enjoyment, and enrichment. For special children, no matter what their disability, music can also be the most important, or even the only, way of reaching them or helping them to learn.

Music Activities for Special Children will show you how music can help teach self-expression, communication and relaxation; how to release tensions; and how to improve motor coordination. Success in performing music can enhance handicapped children's self-esteem and help them develop social relationships when making music with others. Included in this book are activities to involve the children in singing, movement, listening, creating, and playing instruments. Special approaches for emotionally disturbed, learning disabled, hearing impaired, speech impaired, mentally retarded, motor impaired, and visually impaired children are suggested, together with special materials and adaptations.

Classroom teachers and music teachers need to develop confidence in using music in order to bring its benefits to students with various disabilities. The same is true for special education teachers who may have the primary responsibility for all aspects of the education of handicapped children.

To achieve these goals, this book offers:

1. basic information regarding the general and/or musical characteristics of children with various disabilities to help you understand why certain activities or approaches may be needed or useful for the children

2. research findings and the results of experiments, case studies, and experience to give meaning to and purpose for the suggestions

3. specific activities to show how this theory, research, and experience can be applied so that handicapped children not only can be helped to participate in many music activities but also, in some cases, to alleviate some of their symptoms or succeed in other areas of the curriculum

v

In addition, the creative teacher, armed with this theoretical knowledge and background information, will be able to develop his or her own additional activities, music games, and applications.

When using *Music Activities for Special Children*, be aware of the need for flexibility. For example, blind, motor impaired, mentally retarded, and learning disabled children can all derive emotional benefits from many of the same activities suggested for children who are emotionally disturbed. The emotionally disturbed child can be helped to learn aspects of the classroom curriculum, such as reading, arithmetic, basic skills, colors, body parts, and so on, using music activities similar to those described for a learning disabled child. In addition, blind, mentally retarded, and hearing impaired children can enjoy and develop physical coordination from some of the activities suggested for motor impaired children.

For example, if you have a retarded 11-year-old child in your class who has a voice dysfunction and is hyperactive, you can use this book in several ways. First read Chapter 5, "Music for the Educable Mentally Retarded Child," for an understanding, based on research, of the music capabilities of the child as well as for a familiarity with many of the activities—some helpful for teaching basic concepts, others for developing the music potential of the child and his or her ability to participate with others.

Next, you would consult Chapter 9, "Music As an Aid in Speech Remediation," to find special music games, songs, and activities to help the child learn to control voice volume. Then Chapter 2, "Music for the Emotionally Disturbed Child," would give you suggestions for enhancing the child's self-image and helping him or her gain self-control.

Finally, the Correlative Song Chart, a special feature of this book, will give you a list of all the songs in this book that are especially helpful to use up excess energy or to enhance relaxation or to teach basic concepts or to help with speech problems. This chart is an index of all the songs and indicates each skill taught by that song.

In one of my classes of educable mentally retarded children, one of the activities was making folders for song sheets, worksheets, drawings dealing with music, pictures of instruments, and so on. The children were told to decorate the folders any way they liked. Later, when I was putting the folders away for the next lesson, one of them caught my attention. In the center of the cover was drawn a single flower and underneath the child had printed MUSIC IS LUV.

Through music, we can all help to bring this love into the lives of handicapped children.

Ruth Zinar

Table of Contents

Chapter 4

MUSIC FOR THE TRAINABLE MENTALLY RETARDED CHILD

Chapter 5

MUSIC FOR THE EDUCABLE MENTALLY RETARDED CHILD

Chapter 6

MUSIC FOR THE
HEARING-IMPAIRED CHILD

Chapter 7

MUSIC FOR THE
MOTOR-IMPAIRED CHILD

Chapter 8

MUSIC FOR THE
VISUALLY IMPAIRED CHILD

Chapter 9

MUSIC AS AN AID
IN SPEECH REMEDIATION

CORRELATIVE SONG CHART

Name of Song	Chapter	Calming	Movement	One-chord	Two chords	Pentatonic	Elimination Song	Cumulative Song	Body Parts	Name Song	Colors	Direction	Suitable for older children	Limited Range	Learning Verbs	Following Instructions	Ostinato	Mathematics	Aid in Speech
Aloha Oe	2	X											X						
Angel Band, The	5	X			X	X												X	
*Au Clair de la Lune	2	X											X	X					
Betty Barter	9				X									X					X
Bingo	2						X												
Chiapanecas, La	2		X						X				X		X	X			
Cindy	5					X							X						
Counting Song	5	X											X					X	
Damper, The	2		X		X		X					X	X						
Down in the Valley	2	X			X								X						
Drum Song	9													X					X
Duke of York	4		X									X	X						
Dundai	5												X				X		
Elephant Song, The	5												X					X	
Exercise Song	2		X			X	X						X			X			
Farmer in the Dell	5			X		X											X		
Four in a Boat	5																	X	
*Frère Jacques	4			X									X						
Go In and Out the Window	4		X	X				X			X				X	X			

---

*If sung in French, suitable for older children.

CORRELATIVE SONG CHART (Cont.)

Name of Song	Chapter	Calming	Movement	One-chord	Two chords	Pentatonic	Elimination Song	Cumulative Song	Body Parts	Name Song	Colors	Direction	Suitable for older children	Limited Range	Learning Verbs	Following Instructions	Ostinato	Mathematics	Aid in Speech
Goodbye, Old Paint	5	X			X								X	X					
Go Tell Aunt Rhodie	5	X			X									X					
Hokey-Pokey	4		X		X				X				X	X	X	X			
Home on the Range	2	X												X					
How Do You Plant Your Cabbages?	3		X		X				X	X						X			
Hush, Little Baby	2	X			X									X					
Jingle Bells	5													X					
If You Clap Your Hands	4		X						X					X	X	X			
If You're Happy	4		X					X	X						X	X			
Kum-Ba-Yah	2	X											X	X					
Little David	4			X	X									X					
**Little Tommy Tinker	4			X	X									X					
**Little Tommy Tinter	9			X	X									X					X
Liza Jane	4			X	X									X					X
My Bonnie	9																		X
**My Goose	4			X	X									X					
My Hat	2		X		X	X								X					
Merry-Go-Round	9			X															X
Movement Song	2		X		X				X							X	X		
Oh, Bury Me Not	9	X			X									X					X

**If sung as a round, suitable for older children.

CORRELATIVE SONG CHART (Cont.)

Name of Song	Chapter	Calming	Movement	One-chord	Two chords	Pentatonic	Elimination Song	Cumulative Song	Body Parts	Name Song	Colors	Direction	Suitable for older children	Limited Range	Learning Verbs	Following Instructions	Ostinato	Mathematics	Aid in Speech
Oh, How Lovely Is the Evening	2	X			X								X	X					
Oh, Lady Moon	2	X	X																
Old King Cole	5							X											
Old Red Wagon	4		X		X	X		X				X		X	X	X			
On Top of Old Smokey	2	X											X						
Peter Piper (words only)	9																		X
Pick a Bale of Cotton	7		X		X														
Playing the Drum	4		X	X								X		X		X			
Row, Row, Row Your Boat	2		X	X															
Sarasponda	5												X				X		
Scotland's Burning	9				X								X						X
See Singing Suzie	9					X								X					X
Shalom Chaverim	4			X									X						
She'll Be Coming Round the Mountain	5	X						X					X						
Stamp Your Feet	2	X							X			X			X	X			
Swinging Song (1)	3	X										X							
Swinging Song (2)	9	X		X								X							X
***Swing Low, Sweet Chariot	4	X		X		X							X				X		

***Ostinato is in Chapter 5.

CORRELATIVE SONG CHART (Cont.)

Name of Song	Chapter	Calming	Movement	One-chord	Two chords	Pentatonic	Elimination Song	Cumulative Song	Body Parts	Name Song	Colors	Direction	Suitable for older children	Limited Range	Learning Verbs	Following Instructions	Ostinato	Mathematics	Aid in Speech
Ten in the Bed	5				X								X	X				X	
This Old Man	5													X				X	
There's a Hole in the Bottom of the Sea	5				X			X						X					
There's a Hole in the Bucket	4		X		X									X					
***There's a Little Wheel	2	X	X			X											X		
Three Caws	5				X													X	
Tree in the Woods, The	5							X						X					
Under the Spreading Chestnut Tree	2	X				X								X					
Westminster Chimes	9	X												X					X
What is Billy Wearing?	2				X					X	X								
When the Saints Go Marching In	9													X					X
Where, Oh Where is Little Susie?	2				X					X									
Won't You Sit Down?	2				X					X	X								
Working on the Railroad	2		X											X					
Zum-Gali-Gali	5				X									X			X		

***Ostinato is in Chapter 5.

Special Note

The following songs and activities first appeared in *Music in Your Classroom* by Ruth Zinar, Ph.D., Copyright © 1983 by Parker Publishing Company, Inc., West Nyack, New York:
Play the Name; Dance the Name; Activities for the Arhythmic Child; Follow the Tune; Play "Freeze"; Follow the Drum; Follow the Dots to Make a G Clef; Tiptoe and Bend Low; Take Turns Moving to Changing Pitch; Move to the Song; Catch High and Low Balls; Move Your Arms to the Sound of the Pitch; Use Word Chants to Learn Long and Short Vowels; Sing a Song about Long and Short Vowels; Create Pentatonic Songs Using Song Bells; Play Questions and Answers on the Song Bells; Play Pentatonic Duets; Play the Autoharp Using Color Coding; Playing the Swiss Melody Bells; Use a Counting Song to Reinforce Number Recognition; Sing a B Song; Be the Alphabet; Find Your Twin Note; Step Rhythms and Change Places; "There's a Little Wheel"; "My Hat"; "Stamp Your Feet"; "Swinging Song"; "How Do You Plant Your Cabbages?"; "If You're Happy"; "The Tree in the Woods"; "This Old Man."
The author has received permission to use the following material:

From "Reading Language and Reading Music; Is There a Connection," by Ruth Zinar, Copyright © 1976 by Music Educators National Conference. Reprinted by permission from *Music Educators Journal*.

From "Music for the Emotionally Disturbed Child in the Mainstreamed Class," accepted by *Instructor*. Used by permission of The Instructor Publications, Inc.

From "The Language Arts and Music: Recent Research," by Ruth Zinar. Used by permission of *Arizona English Bulletin*.

C H A P T E R ✖ 1

THE EFFECTS OF MUSIC AND ITS ROLE IN SPECIAL EDUCATION

Most of us are aware that music can affect our moods. We know that sometimes it can make repetitive work less tedious, that it can make us feel more relaxed or more cheerful, or less tense and bored. At times, it can start feet tapping and hands moving, or cause nostalgia, longing, or feelings of tenderness.

At the same time that our feelings are being affected, other things are happening to the body which we do not realize.[1] It has been shown, for example, that music can affect blood pressure and heartbeat and can even restore the size of the pupils of eyes fatigued by exposure to light. Respiration rate increases with strong, lively music such as Liszt's "Hungarian Rhapsody, Number Two," and posture is different when people listen to stimulative music than when they listen to serene music.

It should not be surprising then that this power of music to affect mood and physical state has resulted in the fact that for ages music and medicine were inseparable in the minds of men, and that to some of the great philosophers, music was considered to be essential in the education of youth.

BACKGROUND INFORMATION

The story of Saul and David from the Old Testament illustrates the belief in the power of music. We are told:

1

"Now the spirit of the Lord had departed from Saul . . . and an evil spirit from the Lord terrified him. And Saul's servants said unto him, 'Behold now, an evil spirit from God . . . terrifieth thee. . . . Seek out a man who is a skillful player on the harp; and it shall be, when the evil spirit from God cometh upon thee, that he shall play with his hand, and thou shalt be well.

". . . And it came to pass, when the evil spirit from God was upon Saul, that David took the harp and played with his hand; so Saul found relief and it was well with him and the evil spirit departed from him."[2]

Throughout man's history, this association of music and therapy recurs. To the ancient Greeks, Apollo, the god of manly beauty and the sun, was also the god of music and of medicine. The mythological Orpheus was able to make rocks weep and almost succeeded in bringing his wife, Euridice, back to life with the beauty of his lyre music.

In his *Politics*, Aristotle wrote of the power of music, declaring that the emotion created by some music can "excite the soul to mystic frenzy. . . . Those who are influenced by pity or fear and every emotional nature . . . [as a result] are purged and their souls lightened and delighted."[3] Greek theorists believed that melodies based on different scales or combinations of tones had various effects on people: some made them sad and grave; others "enfeebled" the mind; still others made them calm and serene. Indeed, Plato, who agreed that the different types of music had these effects, warned that music must be "preserved in [its] original form and no innovation made. . . ." So powerful can the emotional effects of music be that society must "try in every possible way to prevent . . . youth from even desiring . . . new modes in dance or song. . . ."[4]

To the ancient Chinese, music was born in man's heart: "Whatever moves the soul pours forth in tones; and again, whatever sounds affect[s] man's soul."[5] Thus, all sound, especially music, was a potent force in the lives of people. The ancient Arabs also believed in the efficacy of music as a healer. Certain melodies healed the eyes; others, palpitations of the heart; others were good for headaches; and some for colic, heart disease, or colds.

In the Middle Ages, following—and probably resulting from—the Great Plague that killed almost one third of the population of Europe, a form of hysteria called the "dancing mania" seized many people. Groups of men and women would grasp hands and dance wildly until they dropped from exhaustion. It was eventually found that when music keeping time to the dance was played for them and then suddenly stopped, they would stop dancing. Or when strong, fast, rhythmic music was played to the rhythm of their dancing and then gradually became slower and quieter, it would bring the dancing episode to a close. Today, we know from scientific studies that the same technique of gradually lessening the intensity of music until it is sedative can be of value in the classroom.

The past century has seen the development of new roles for music in medicine, in therapy, and in education. In medicine, music is used in the dentist's office to lessen tension and to distract from the noise of the drill. It is also used to lessen pain and discomfort following surgery and as an adjunct to anesthesia. At Kaiser Permanente Medical Center in Los Angeles and at the University of Massachusetts, music has been used to aid relaxation in stress management.[6] At the University of Kansas Medical Center, it has been played during labor and childbirth to shorten delivery time.[7]

From its first use in mental hospitals as recreational therapy or as an adjunct in occupational therapy, music has, since the end of World War II, become an additional tool in restoring physical and emotional health as well as playing a significant role in the education of the handicapped child. The use of music to aid the handicapped child is supported by the results of numerous studies and experiments on the effects of music on emotions and on learning. (A number of these, together with their applications to the classroom, are described in relevant chapters of this book.)

It has been found, for example, that children draw different types of pictures to sedative than to stimulating music, and that when a series of compositions of various moods are played, there is a change of mood in the listeners to the direction of the mood of the music. Sometimes, a mood can be intensified. Thus, it is inadvisable to play mournful, tragic works, such as the slow movement of Tchaikowsky's *Symphonie Pathetique*, for people who were already fatigued or depressed.[8]

In one study, one hundred college students wearing blindfold goggles were given a pencil maze to solve, then told that they were incorrect and to try again. This was repeated until measurements of the increased moisture of the skin showed increased anxiety. This was done with and without music in the background. It was found that with the music, there was a significant reduction in the anxiety levels, the music serving as an emotional release and an outlet for tension.[9] How many children have used this technique, listening to their favorite music, to make doing homework less burdensome and tension-producing?

Various theories have been advanced for the physical and emotional effects of music. Not only do they help to explain why music is such a potent force in the education of all children, but they also show why it is especially valuable for those who are handicapped. Do our moods affect our bodies? Do our bodies affect our moods? Does music change the functions of our bodies and hence our moods? Or does it change our moods and thus influence our bodies? The answers are not known, but can only be surmised. Some of the theories, all of which have implications for education, are as follows.

It is known that there is a rhythm in the brain called "brain waves" and that it can be influenced by mental and physical states. Music rhythm can affect brain rhythm and thus affect mood and autonomic physical response.[10] What is more, music rhythms can stimulate unconscious responses in the thalamus, ". . . the seat of sensations and emotions."[11] Without being aware of it, autonomic functions of the body are affected by music and this, in turn, can influence and alter the child's thoughts and feelings.

The left side of the brain is involved in reading and writing, the right side in apprehending melody and appreciating a song. Thus, when we sing or read music, both sides of the brain are involved. This means that in the classroom, we can call upon and involve more of the child's potential.

Another theory sees music's influence as stemming from the very start of life when the infant in the uterus feels the mother's heartbeat and the rhythms of her body. Thus, music can give a feeling of security and a sense of being cared for. This can have implications in the choice of music for the classroom.

At the same time, music has the ability to impel people to move. Start to sing a rousing spiritual with guitar accompaniment or play a recording of a gospel song and start to clap your hands. In a group of disparate people who barely know each other, most of them will soon be tapping feet, singing, or moving together. This factor can influence children's moods and the teacher's ability to get them to work together.

Some theorists believe that the reaction of the human organism to music is based on reactions to the physical laws of acoustics and the various ratios which exist between different melodic and harmonic intervals or combinations of tones.[12]

Whatever theory or theories one accepts regarding the reasons for music's physical and emotional effects, these effects can, in turn, affect the mood and climate of the classroom. A nonverbal form of communication, music meets the aesthetic need for beauty of sound. It can help to provide opportunity for noncompetitive achievement. Removed from everyday problems, its very structure and form can provide order and security in a disturbed child's chaotic life. For all children, it can soothe or stimulate. As "fun," it increases the attention span in learning other areas of the curriculum. Capable of reaching the emotions, it can be an aid in getting children to work together, move together, and play together.

MUSIC IN SPECIAL EDUCATION

PL 94-142, the "Equal Educational Accessibility" (EEA) laws, signed into law by President Ford in 1975, did more than provide that a free public education in the least restrictive environment be made available to all handicapped children. It also specified that consultations among parents, teachers, psychologists, and physicians are required to set up an Individualized Educational Program (IEP) for each child which, taking into consideration the child's needs, potential, and disabilities, would include a statement of goals and the services to be provided to help reach those goals.[13]

Among such related services are transportation, psychological services, physical and/or occupational therapy, counseling, recreation, and medical services. The supportive services also include artistic and cultural programs such as art, music, and dance therapy if they can assist a child to benefit from special education.[14] The same variety of educational programs and services available to nonhandicapped children, including art and music, must be made available to the handicapped child. This was deemed essential because the arts cannot only teach special skills but also, according to those who framed the laws, "the integration of the arts into curriculum for these children is an important consideration that educational programs should not overlook. It may well be that using the arts as a vehicle for instruction could benefit the child where other instructional approaches have not been successful."[15]

The reasons the special child can especially benefit from music are manifold. First of all, music can be taught in a noncompetitive way. Whether a child is severely retarded or physically handicapped, he can enjoy music and be able to participate together with others.

Not only can all children achieve some success in some way in music, but practically all respond to it. As an illustration of this, one teacher reports that in her special class there was a three-year-old autistic girl who never showed any interest or indication that she was aware of what was happening around her. One day, the teacher, who was learning to play the recorder, brought the instrument into school and played it for the children. A somewhat inept performer, the teacher had trouble keeping a steady rhythm and so, as she played, she would tap her foot vigorously and bob her body up and down as an aid. When she finished playing a little tune she had learned, all the children were invited to hold the recorder and to try to "play" it. The autistic child approached, took the instrument in hand and began to blow into it. But as she did, she imitated the teacher, tapping her foot and bobbing her body in the same way. Obviously, she had noticed her surroundings; the music called forth the first overt response.

These physical and emotional effects of music help to make music different from other subject areas in the curriculum of the special child. At the same time that the children can be learning something about music, listening to music, or participating in making music, other goals can be equally important for the special children. Music for these youngsters is used to help the child communicate, whether the problem is an emotionally disturbed child having difficulty expressing his feelings or a trainable retarded child learning a basic language vocabulary. It is used to lessen tensions and to aid relaxation. It is used to enhance the child's self-esteem—perhaps, for a severely retarded child, to learn his or her name and that he or she has an identity, or for one with a learning disability, to feel capable of achievement in music equal to that of others in the class. For the physically handicapped—the hearing impaired, motor handicapped, and visually impaired—it can help to overcome fear of movement, improve motor coordination, and enable the child to participate with other children.

For all children, it makes a difference if you use music to teach other subjects, because music makes learning easier. Through the use of appropriate materials, music can enhance instruction by making it more vivid, more concrete, and more varied. The multi-sense approach possible (and indeed, even necessary) in teaching music helps to make learning more fun, and what is learned more enjoyably is more easily remembered.

Unfortunately, too many classroom teachers feel insecure about teaching music at all, and many music teachers have that same insecurity when it comes to teaching music to special children.[16] Actually, it is not necessary for the classroom or the special education teacher to be a trained musician in order to *use* many music activities to help the handicapped child. And the music teacher, with guidance and knowledge about special children, can be aided in developing a suitable program to teach music to them.

Basically, the differences between music for the average child and music for the special child lie in several areas: The activities and materials may be the same for the handicapped child as for the non-handicapped, but especially selected to meet special needs. The basic activities may be the same, but the materials adapted in some way to enable the handicapped child to participate and succeed. The materials may be the same, but the activities adapted to some extent. And finally, special materials and activities may need to be developed to help reach the desired goals.

In short, for the special child, music is *not just taught* for its own sake. It is also *used* to achieve desired goals beyond the music, to aid in emotional health and to assist in other areas of learning. "All children have the need for expression through music, but for the handicapped child, the physical, emotional, and intellectual benefits that can be derived from music make it an essential part of classroom activities."[17]

SUMMARY

Throughout history, the ability of music to exhilarate or to calm was recognized, and many myths and legends about the curative powers of music grew up as a result. Today, scientific studies have proved that music affects mood and many functions of the body, including rate of breathing, blood pressure, size of the pupils of the eyes, awareness of pain, and heartbeat. It can also aid learning, ease childbirth, and lessen anxiety.

The reasons for these effects are not known, but a number of theories have been suggested. Brain waves are known to be affected by music and brain waves, in turn, can affect mood. The "split brain" theory suggests that reading music involves both right and left sides of the brain. Some believe that prenatal rhythms sensed by the unborn child sensitize an individual to similar rhythms in the environment. Music can also stimulate people, getting them to move, and in the case of some songs, evoke nostalgia and "tender emotions" of love, compassion, and caring.

Music plays an important role in Special Education, not only because of its ability to soothe or to stimulate, but because it makes instruction in other areas of the curriculum more vivid, more concrete, more varied, and more enjoyable. Sometimes, it is the only way some children can learn.

Music can help all children communicate. It can aid in relaxation and achievement and can enhance the child's self-image. Regardless of impairment, every child can participate and achieve in some way through music.

NOTES

[1]Max Schoen, editor. *The Effects of Music.* Freeport, New York: Books for Libraries Press, reprinted 1968.

[2]*Old Testament*, First Samuel; 16.

[3]Aristotle. *Politics, Book VIII, 7.*

[4]Plato. *Laws, VII.*

[5]Curt Sachs. *The Rise of Music in the Ancient World.* (New York: W.W. Norton and Company, 1943), p. 106. Citing Lü Pu-We, *Shi-Ch'un Ts-u*, third century, B.C.

[6]Rick McGuire. "Taking Note of Music as Medical Aid." *Los Angeles Times* (March 27, 1984), Part V, pp. 1–2.

[7]Clark, Michael, et al. "Music Therapy Assisted Labor and Delivery." *Journal of Music Therapy*, 18, No. 2 (Summer, 1981), pp. 88–100.

[8]*The Effects of Music*, pp. 195–96.

[9]Peter O. Peretti and Kathy Swenson. "Effects of Music on Anxiety as Determined by Physiological Skin Responses." *Journal of Research in Music Education*, 22, No. 4. (Winter, 1974), pp. 278–83.

[10]George A. Giacobbe. "Rhythm Builds Order in Brain-Damaged Children," in *Music in Special Education.* Washington, D.C.: Music Educators National Conference, 1972, pp. 24–27.

[11]Giacobbe. "Rhythm Builds Order," p. 25.

[12]Paul Farnsworth. *The Social Psychology of Music.* New York: Holt, Rinehart and Winston, 1958, pp. 35–54.

[13]Richard M. Graham and Alice S. Beer. *Teaching Music to the Exceptional Child.* Englewood Cliffs, New Jersey: Prentice-Hall, Inc., 1980, p. 13.

[14]Public Law 94-142, Sec. 121a.13, 1975.

[15]"Related Services in the IEP," *News Briefs*, 2, No. 3. (June, 1979). Office for Education of Children with Handicapping Conditions, New York State Department of Education.

[16]Melanie Stuart and Janet Gilbert. "Mainstreaming: Needs Assessment Through a Videotape Visual Scale." *Journal of Research in Music Education*, 25, No. 4. (Winter, 1977), pp. 283–89.

[17]Ruth Zinar. "Music in the Mainstream." *Teacher*, 96, No. 7, (March, 1978), p. 56.

CHAPTER ✕ 2

MUSIC FOR THE
EMOTIONALLY DISTURBED CHILD

They fight with each other; call out; make faces and insulting remarks; hit; cry; throw tantrums, pencils, and paper clips; clown; sulk; and interfere with instruction. In music class, they might deliberately play out of rhythm or sing off-key or make up their own words (including some startling obscenities) to a song. Some of them show none of these symptoms, but instead, are withdrawn.

Unable to fully function intellectually or in relationship to others, they are the emotionally disturbed and they make up at least two percent of the school population (about one and a quarter million children).[1] The Office of Education of the Department of Health, Education, and Welfare further described emotionally disturbed children: there is, in addition to "an ability to learn which cannot be explained by intellectual, sensory, or health factors," a general feeling of unhappiness and a tendency toward developing school phobias or physical symptoms.

The reactions of some emotionally disturbed children to music they hear seem to differ from those of normal children. When asked if a large variety of orchestral pieces played for them were happy or sad, liked or disliked, good or bad, both normal and aggressive, emotionally disturbed boys, nine to twelve years of age and with normal intelligence, liked or disliked the same music and perceived the same music as being "happy." However, the emotionally disturbed youngsters did not see music as being "sad" as often (perhaps, showing lack of empathy) and their answers were more erratic than those of normal children.[2] Overt responses to music are also more unpredict-

able. For example, in one music class, when a lilting cowboy song
was played to a group of emotionally disturbed boys, one clapped his
hands vigorously and rapidly, one glowered at the teacher, one put
his thumb in his mouth, and one promptly stretched out on several
chairs and went to sleep.

No wonder most teachers find the emotionally disturbed difficult
to teach. Although it might be best to have them in classes with a
maximum of about eight pupils, this is not always possible. Federal
mandates for mainstreaming and lack of funds or facilities all add up
to the fact that many troubled youngsters can be found in the regular classroom. Fortunately, they can be helped through music
because it is a nonthreatening, nonverbal form of communication
that can establish relationships. In a music class, children can express a variety of emotions as they sing. At the same time, they are
learning to express them in a controlled, acceptable way. If experiences in music can be provided which call forth positive responses,
similar responses may result in other situations. In order for there to
be progress in behavior, communication, and socialization, however,
the attitude that music is meant to be enjoyed must be created, not
criticized or judged. Release of tension, the development of an improved self-image, and, incidentally, some knowledge of music can
result from music activities.

RESEARCH FINDINGS

A number of studies by music therapists, psychiatrists, and psychologists not only highlight the benefits of music for the emotionally disturbed, but also suggest techniques which can be helpful to those
teachers in whose classrooms many of those troubled children can
and will be found in increasing numbers.

In one study, "vocal dynamics" were used with patients in a
psychiatric hospital, most of them in their late teens and early twen-
ties.[3] During these vocal dynamics sessions, exercises involving the
body and voice were used to indicate feelings and to produce sound:
"fast and slow," "weak and strong," "loud and soft," "passive and
aggressive" were expressed through body movement and through
the use of neutral sounds like the letters of the alphabet or numbers.
This activity helped the patients to relax and to move freely, and as
a result, they were able to communicate more easily with each other
and with the therapists.

In another study used with adult patients participating in group therapy, having them sing with each other made them less defensive and they were able to allow themselves to relate in more meaningful ways.[4] They also began to bring in cassettes of their favorite music to share, and they discussed the reactions and feelings evoked by the music. Music used this way in psychotherapy has been found to create or alter moods and to aid in exploring feelings.

The same enhancement of group feeling occurred with hospitalized adolescents suffering from adjustment reactions.[5] The experimental group attended music therapy sessions in which they listened to music, discussed their reactions to the moods of the music, and created stories and drew to the music. The control group had no music therapy. Pretests and post-tests in self-esteem, agreement about the mood or emotion expressed in the music, and the use of pronouns (I, me, my, mine, as contrasted with we, our, us, ours) as well as sociograms revealed significant differences in favor of the experimental subjects. They did not use the first person singular as often but rather spoke more of "we" and "us." Group cohesion was more evident and there was also some improvement in self-esteem noted for those who had participated in the music therapy sessions.

According to some behavioral therapists, some of the effects of music stem from the fact that parents the world over have sung to their children in providing and caring for them, so that to most infants, music is associated with food, water, shelter, or with the mother singing a gentle lullabye.[6] Thus, songs which have lyrics dealing with such aspects of life as love, loyalty, or unity can help to create and maintain pleasant and useful group interaction. These therapists believe that it is essential for music to have lyrics relevant to solving personal problems in everyday life in order for it to be therapeutic.

Most therapists, however, do not agree with the opinion that lyrics are essential. Dorothy Brin Crocker, for example, found that when children tell stories of their own creating to music, this can reveal disturbed feelings.[7] Juliette Alvin tells of a very disturbed child who imagined herself searching through the woods for some "thing" unknown. At last, she found a little baby doll hidden under the leaves; so she picked it up and started to eat it.[8]

Crocker also found that the children with whom she worked grew to associate feelings and special activities with specific music titles and sounds. Thus, the chord progression V^7–I meant "Sit down," and special music came to mean "Form a circle for a game." Improvised music given the titles "Anger" or "Fear" helped the children to talk more freely about these emotions whenever they heard the music played. In one incident, for example, two emotionally disturbed boys began to fight with another who had been the aggressor. Without a word "fight music" was played and then quickly changed to the "form a circle" melody. The class responded at once. The circle was formed, the fight was over.

As a result of an experiment with three emotionally disturbed boys who exhibited very disruptive behavior (calling out, hitting, crying, tantrums, making nonverbal noises, destructiveness, and hyperactivity), it was found that deprivation of listening to music can be used to modify behavior.[9] In this study, background music was played as the boys did other class work and it was stopped if any of them misbehaved. Specific rules of behavior were established (e.g., staying in the seat, no calling out, no hitting). In order for the music to be started again, all three had to be following the rules. By about the twenty-fifth session, there was an obvious improvement in behavior. Group pressure began to be exerted. When a youngster broke a rule, causing the music to stop, there would be protests: "Keep quiet, I want to listen!" "You made her turn the music off!" "Come on, we can't hear the music when you do that." The desire to hear the background music increased adherence to rules and led to more cooperation. These results were duplicated when music played for children riding in a school bus was stopped for five seconds every time one of them got out of his/her seat. In short order, they were all staying put![10]

At Northern University, another aspect of music instruction—instrument lessons—was tried in a special music program for two classes, each with six emotionally disturbed boys, six to ten years of age.[11] These children were hyperactive or withdrawn, displaying temper outbursts and physical or verbal aggression. They were taught to play the harp or the piano and the instruction was designed so that the children experienced immediate success. There were color coding, simplified notation, and special construction for the harp. On the piano, the keys were lettered and the keyboard shortened and very simple ensemble arrangements were written so that the sound was satisfying at the earliest level. The youngsters had headphones to use individually and later, works were performed as duets, trios, or quartets. Those who were capable enough were taught traditional notation. A system of "points" for each positive behavior (e.g., following instructions, paying attention, completing a task) was established. These were converted into rewards such as lunch with the teacher or being a monitor.

The music teachers found that not only did the children make progress in learning the instruments, but they showed significant improvement in insight and cooperation and evidenced better self-control.

A number of efforts to determine whether music can help to alleviate hyperactivity in both the emotionally disturbed and the normal child have reached similar conclusions: Three out of four hyperactive pupils were quieter when background music was added to the classroom.[12]

When soothing background music was played for normal third graders of different intelligence levels, although this had no effect on talking, crying, giggling, daydreaming, or standing, there was less observed behavior indicating tension—whistling, quarrels, and destructive behavior. It was especially useful in lessening tics and for times the children were supposed to be working quietly doing activities such as written work, small group reading, silent reading, and story hours.[13]

A gradual change in background music from lively, popular to "sedative" (i.e., calm, lyrical) was played for normally behaved children of various mathematical abilities. The result was a trend towards greater mathematical achievement for the slower pupils and the brighter ones responded equally well with only soft background music. The important finding was that all the children reported feeling more rested and all experienced more pleasant feelings when they had the music.[14]

Similarly, this gradual change from stimulating, rhythmic, strong music to sedative music resulted in improved behavior in emotionally disturbed children.[15]

Some researchers hypothesized that quiet activities and low stimulation tend to make the hyperactive more restless. Thus, stimulants such as drugs and caffeine have sometimes been used to quiet them. But when an ascending music stimulus program (starting with serene music and gradually changing to livelier and stronger "pop" music) was used with second and third graders, more hyperactivity resulted.[16] This and the other studies indicate that quiet music or a gradual change to quiet music is most useful in creating a calmer atmosphere in the classroom.

In addition to all of the effects of music just described, it has been shown that music used as a *reward* for good behavior has been an effective tool in creating a favorable classroom atmosphere.[17]

Thus, as we can see, music therapy and appropriate music activities apparently can help to alleviate symptoms in the emotionally disturbed child. Used as an adjunct in the classroom, it can help to improve self-image, aid in communication and expression of feelings, help to relieve tension and to build relationships with others.

MUSIC ACTIVITIES

Because music reaches the emotions, it can be a valuable tool in working with the emotionally disturbed. We have seen how various types of music activities have been successfully used with emotionally disturbed children and adults. It is possible to modify these activities and to use other approaches when teaching the emotionally disturbed in the classroom. All of the suggested activities can be excellent for all children; for the emotionally disturbed, they are used primarily to modify behavior. If music skills are developed, this is done not only for their own sake, but to help the child cope with his feelings and his world.

Activities for Enhancing Self-Esteem

1. Whenever possible, have the emotionally disturbed youngsters help others during music activities. They can, for example, become the "music partners" of physically handicapped children, holding the drum or drumstick. Older children can aid by moving a wheelchair in time to the music, or gently helping the physically handicapped to clap where this is needed. The ego enhancement which can result from assisting others and the feeling of importance can carry over to other areas.

2. Let the emotionally disturbed pupil be the "instrument monitor" *if and when* suitable behavior is manifested. This can be a reward when an improvement in cooperation is noted.

3. Provide for success, as was done in the study at Northern University. For this, it is not necessary to have pianos or harps in the elementary classroom. Some classroom instruments (autoharps and melody bells) can be used with color coding where necessary and suitable. Examples of this can be seen in the many musical toys avail-

able which come with music and have the notes in color—a special color for each note. A bar or key of the instrument represented by that note has the same color so that the child is able to locate the correct tune.

This same sort of approach can be used for pupils in the intermediate and upper grades who are learning to play instruments of band or orchestra and who need help to raise self-esteem. Music lessons for them should provide for success through simple step-by-step procedures and/or, if necessary, simplifying the music. In these cases, the degree to which the music is simplified or arranged would, of course, depend on the child's innate musicality and intellectual ability. Brighter children need challenge. Children who have more difficulty in learning, whether because of a learning disability or mental retardation, need special help. (For detailed suggestions for helping children with these handicaps achieve in music, see the relevant chapters.)

4. Give the emotionally disturbed child a special role to play in music class. This has helped many youngsters. Dennis, for example, was a very troubled fifth grade boy of twelve who never learned to play the recorder and was frequently disruptive in class, calling out and constantly interrupting. An accompaniment was needed for a recorder performance of "The Trolley Song," and his jazzy syncopated drum playing was chosen. At the end of the performance he said, "Thank you for letting me play the drum," and the teacher, in genuine surprise at *his* thanking *her*, replied, "Thank *you* for playing so well. I picked you to play because you did it the best."

After that, when he started to be disruptive, the music teacher had only to look at him and to murmur in a slightly wounded tone, "Dennis." He would say, "All right—I'll be good!" and he would be. Undoubtedly, the success he experienced (perhaps the only time he had been praised for doing well) was responsible for this change.

5. If the class is given the opportunity to improvise using rhythm instruments or to have a creative "jam" session, let the emotionally disturbed child have a chance to be the soloist or the conductor. Because in improvisations one can create one's own sounds with the instrument, there should be no judgments and no competition. Hence, in this and in all the other activities in which the goal is to enhance self-esteem through creating, the teacher's attitude should be that there are no errors.

Adolescents enjoy improvising rhythms on percussion instruments, and most of the rhythm band activities described here and in other parts of this book are fine for them. Make sure, however, that for them the instruments used are "real" ones or as much like those used in the school band or orchestra as possible.

6. Use "name games." These can be very successful in giving a pupil a feeling of being important. This can be done through the use of body movement or rhythm instruments, playing a "talking drum," or a tune on the black bars of resonator or song bells.

Play the name: Ask the child to say his name and then repeatedly clap or play the rhythmic pattern of the name. Have the children join you. Most children are delighted to hear their names transformed into music, and a number of attractive rhythm patterns played on various instruments will result in a variety of attractive sounds.

Dance the name: Have all the children stand and clap the rhythm of a name several times: e.g., Mo-ni-ca Thomp--son

Then have them dance in place to the tapping out of the rhythm.

Sing songs using the child's name: You can expect that children will usually be delighted to hear their names included in a song, or else to have a special song all for themselves. Just use the name of the child about whom you are singing in place of the name in the music score:

WHAT IS BILLY WEARING?

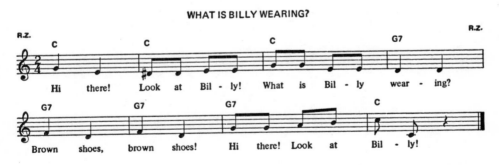

Sing additional verses about other children and other colors—Patty's wearing white sneakers, Darryl's wearing a blue shirt, and so on.

WONT' YOU SIT DOWN?

Who's that yon-der dressed in red, Must be lit-tle (child's name) she's the best, I said. O won't you sit down? No, I can't sit down 'Cause I _____ just got here, got to look a-round.

WHERE, OH WHERE IS LITTLE SUSIE?

1. Where, oh where, is lit-tle Su-sie,
2. Come on, boys, and let's go find her,

Where oh where, is lit-tle Su-sie,
Come on, boys, and let's go find her,

Where oh where, is lit-tle Su-sie,
Come on, boys, and let's go find her,

Way down yon-der in the paw-paw patch.
Way down yon-der in the paw-paw patch.

3. Pickin' up pawpaws, put 'em in a basket,
   Pickin' up pawpaws, put 'em in a basket.
   Pickin' up pawpaws, put 'em in a basket.
   Way down yonder in the pawpaw patch.

Activities to Aid in Relaxation and/or Release of Tension

1. You may find that three out of four hyperactive pupils in your classes are quieter and work more productively when background music is added; and this has been the experience of many teachers. For a calming influence, try using soft background music as the children do imitative paper work. Do not expect any carry-over to other periods, however, or a buildup of beneficial effects. Background music (we hear it in supermarkets, department stores, or elevators) has become so much a part of the environment that we hardly notice it consciously. For all ages, it does help to make waiting less boring, work less tedious, and surroundings less anxiety-producing.

2. Have the children pass a bean bag or jingle bells (using the bean bag if there are children who may throw the bells with intent to hurt) or play rhythm instruments to the beat of moderately slow dance music. A Greek slow "Hosopikos" or a Latin American "Cha-Cha" would be appropriate. These are relaxing and pleasant activities; none of them are demanding, and the tempo and beat of the music enhances an easy-going feeling. Teenagers can enjoy playing along with the maracas, claves, castenets, etc.

3. Add gestures to a moderately slow, relaxed song, such as "There's a Little Wheel."

THERE'S A LITTLE WHEEL

American Folk Song

This is a quiet, restful song and the motions should therefore be done gently.

Words	Motions
There's a little wheel a-turning in my heart.	Wind or turn hands around each other.
In my heart, in my heart. . . .	Clasp both hands to heart.

"Oh, Lady Moon" is also suitable for slow, gentle movements:

OH, LADY MOON

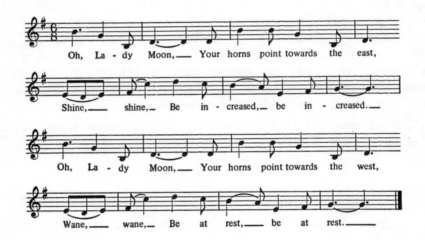

Words	Motions
Oh, Lady Moon, Your horns point towards the east,	Arms encircled above head.
Shine, shine, Be increased, be increased.	Gradually extend arms and bring slowly to the side.
Oh, Lady Moon, Your horns point towards the west,	Arms encircled above head.
Wane, wane,	Gradually lower arms and fold hands.
Be at rest, be at rest.	Bow head towards hands, eyes closed.

4. Have a large repertoire of restful, lilting, lyrical songs, including lullabyes. There are hundreds of these to choose from and they include songs suitable for many grade levels. Among them are:

DOWN IN THE VALLEY

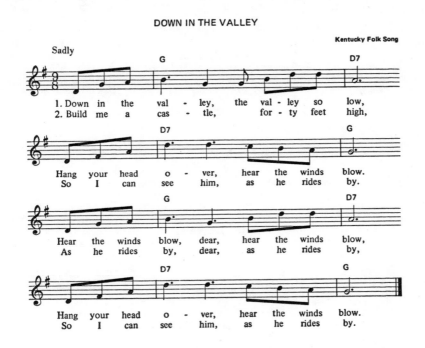

ON TOP OF OLD SMOKY

3. He'll love you and leave you,
   And tell you more lies,
   Than trees in a forest,
   Or stars in the skies.

4. Repeat first stanza.

KUM-BA—YAH

2. Someone's singing, Lord . . .

3. Someone's praying, Lord . . .

(Children can make up additional verses.)

HUSH, LITTLE BABY

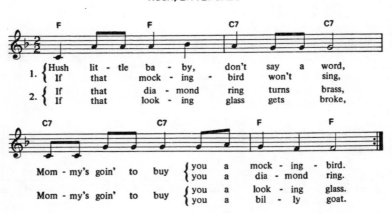

3. If that billy goat won't pull,
   Mommy's goin' to buy you a cart and bull.
   If that cart and bull turn over,
   Mommy's goin' to buy you a dog named Rover.

4. If that Rover dog won't bark,
   Mommy's goin' to buy you a horse and cart.
   If that horse and cart break down,
   You'll still be the sweetest little baby in town.

HOME ON THE RANGE

Brewster Higley (1873)   Cowboy, U.S.A.

Oh,___ give me a home where the buf - fa - lo roam, Where the
Where the air is so pure and the zeph - yrs so free, And the

deer and the an - te - lope play,___ Where_ sel - dom is heard a dis-
breez - es so balm - y and light,___ That I would not ex - change my___

cour - ag - ing word, And the skies are not cloud - y all day.___
home on the range, For___ all of the cit - ies so bright.___

Refrain:

Home, home on the range,___ Where the deer and the

an - te - lope play,___ Where sel - dom is heard a dis-

cour - ag - ing word, And the skies are not cloud - y all day.___

ALÒHA-OE

English version by R.Z.   Queen Liliuokalani

From these love - ly is - lands in the sea ___ Our ship is

bear-ing us a - way. ___ Tho' we say our sad fare - wells to

thee, ___ Still we know that we will re - turn some - day. ___

ALÒHA-OE (Cont.)

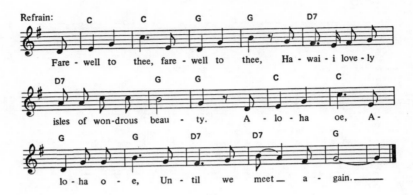

Fare - well to thee, fare - well to thee, Ha - wai - i love - ly
isles of won-drous beau - ty. A - lo - ha oe, A -
lo - ha o - e, Un - til we meet — a - gain.

AU CLAIR DE LA LUNE

1. Au clair de la lu - ne, Mon a - mi Pier - rot,
2. Au clair de la lu - ne, Pier - rot ré - pon dit,

Prê - te - moi ta plu - me, Pour é - crire un mot.
"Je n'ai pas de plu - me, Je suis dans mon lit.

Ma chan-delle est mor - te, Je n'ai plus de feu;
Va chez la voi - si - ne, Je crois qu'elle y est,

Ou - vre - moi ta por - te, Pour l'a - mour de Dieu.
Car dans sa cui - si - ne, On bat le bri - quet."

Literal translation

Verse 1:

By the light of the moon,
My friend, Pierrot,
Lend me a pen
To write a word.
My candle has gone out,
I have no more fire,
Open your door to me,
For goodness' sake.

English Version

By the silv'ry moonlight,
I ask Pierrot, my friend,
"Do you have a pencil,
That to me you'll lend?
My poor candle's gone out,
And I cannot see,
Open up your door, then,
Give a light to me."

Literal translation	*English Version*
Verse 2:	
By the light of the moon	By the silv'ry moonlight
Pierrot replied,	Pierrot to me said,
"I don't have a pen,	"I don't have a pencil,
I'm in my bed.	And I'm still in bed.
Go to the neighbor,	Go and try our neighbor,
I think she's there,	For I think she's there.
For in her kitchen,	From her kitchen window,
Someone strikes a light."	A light is shining clear."

OH, HOW LOVELY IS THE EVENING

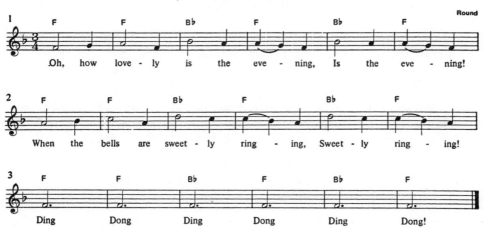

5. Use the vocal dynamics exercise. This is an enjoyable and fine activity for having fun and relieving tensions, and it can be done in this way: Tell the children to repeat the alphabet in time to a drum beat (or accompanied by the piano), but as they do so, they are to pretend to be very angry. Or they can express this "anger" by body movements (e.g., waving arms, stamping, striking the air) and simultaneous loud counting. The important rule here is that there is to be no hitting and no touching of anyone or anything.

6. Play the autoharp or guitar to accompany the songs. Very often, these instruments can be much better than the piano because the teacher can face the class and the children can sit near the teacher. The closeness that results can give the children a feeling of security. For the classroom teacher who cannot play either the piano

or guitar, the autoharp (see Figure 2-1) is very simple to learn. It is played by simultaneously pressing a button indicating the name of the desired chord and strumming the strings:

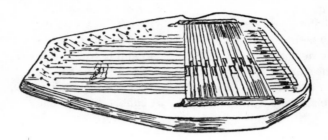

Figure 2-1

7. If you can play the flute or the recorder, its sweet, gentle tones in the lower register are very soothing and calming.

8. Have a large variety of songs, including those that can relax as well as those that can stimulate. It is important to avoid lyrics that could have words with disturbing or unhappy associations for the child. For example, the old Appalachian folk song, "Go Tell Aunt Rhodie," can be amusing to most children as they sing:

> Go tell Aunt Rhodie . . . her old gray goose is dead.
> The one she was saving . . . to make a feather bed.
> The goslings are crying . . . because their mother's dead.

But for the child who has either a fear of losing or a feeling of hostility towards a mother, these words can be deeply disturbing. Learning about the problems and background of the maladjusted child might help to avoid any song which could possibly antagonize him or cause a disruption in class.

9. Avoid sudden, loud noises and be sure to keep your voice well regulated, without any high-pitched "screaming." These can only result in increasing the tensions of a sensitive child.

10. If the mood of a class is chaotic and disturbed, use body movement activities and gesture songs to release tensions, rather than giving a lesson in music notation or teaching an instrument.

11. Have available in back of the room a "music corner" with record player and earphones, and recordings for those times when the disturbed child may have trouble listening to music with others or when the hyperactive child, finished with assigned work, cannot re-

main seated. In this way, the need for his own special music can be met and he can listen without distracting the other children. The music corner can also be equipped with illustrated books about music and pictures of instruments, composers, performers, etc. The pupil can cut out and paste these into a class music scrapbook.

12. When selecting songs or listening material for the class, match the music you play or have the class sing to the disturbed child's mood and then gradually change the music to the desired mood. If the child is tearful or sad, start with quiet, sweet music (e.g., "The Swan" by St. Saens) and then play several recordings, each one a little livelier, ending, perhaps, with the "Can-Can" music from Offenbach's "Gaités Parisiennes" or a Scott Joplin ragtime piece.

On the other hand, if the class is over-excited or if there has been a fight or one appears to be imminent, have them sing a strong rhythmic, rousing song with motions such as "I've Been Working on the Railroad" or "Drill, Ye Tarriers, Drill" and follow with several songs, each one quieter, ending with one like "Santa Lucia," "Hush, Little Baby," or "Kum-Ba-Yah." This approach can be particularly helpful in calming or soothing distressed or over-excited feelings.

13. Teach songs with refrains. The recurring melody and words add to the enjoyment of singing and also give to some children a feeling of security. Just as adults may feel strange the first night in a new place but begin to feel "at home" the second or third night, children can feel at home with the music and be delighted and reassured by the refrain.

14. In planning music activities, it is usually wise to start with some kind of directed activity—singing a greeting song, engaging in an activity requiring sharing instruments, or singing several familiar songs. This can be followed with free improvisations for release of tensions. If you start with free, individualized improvisations, the children may get too excited and things may become out of control.

Activities to Aid in Communication and Self-Expression

1. Among the best loved music activities are music dramatization and drawing or painting to music. Not only are they fun, but they can provide a useful physical outlet and emotional release from inhibitions. As the class listens to music that has clearly obvious moods, they can dance, pantomime, or draw to express how the music

makes them feel or what they are thinking of. Such works as "Baba Yaga" or "Gnomus" from Mussorgsky's *Pictures at an Exhibition*, "Sabre Dance" by Katchaturian, St. Saens' "The Swan," or "Bacarolle" by Offenbach are among the many compositions suitable for these activities.

The pictures the children draw or their conceptions of the "Gnome" or of "Baba Yaga" (a witch so ugly, she hid all the time in a little hut that ran around on chicken legs) may surprise you. During one such music period, while most of the children drew to "The Swan" pictures of flowers, birds floating on the water, or figures dancing, one little boy drew a tombstone with a crying figure standing nearby. The tombstone had his own name on it. Another child drew children crying "Boo-hoo! Boo-hoo! We lost our mother." (Of course, where this type of self-expression is the goal, the children should not be told what the music is about.) If you should observe these types of responses, let the case worker, therapist, or school psychologist see the pictures in order to be able to have more insight into what might be troubling the children.

Through such techniques as these, the children are frequently helped to express disturbed thoughts and emotions.

2. Instead of "acting out" the music or drawing to it, the children can discuss their reactions to the music. For those who find it difficult to express their feelings, the discussion can start objectively with such questions as: "Was this music fast or slow?" "Was it Presto or Allegro?" "Which instrument played the middle part?" Then the mood of the music—whether it was sad, or happy, or excited, or upset, etc.—can be discussed; and finally, it may be possible to elicit responses to such questions as"How did the music make you feel?"

3. The class can also write or tell stories suggested by the music. Similar to drawing or painting to music, this activity uses a different creative medium.

4. A variation of the "vocal dynamics" exercise can be used. Various emotions and feelings—hostility, sadness, loneliness, shyness, aggressiveness—can be expressed verbally and with body movement to appropriate drum or piano accompaniment. These exercises could help to develop the feel of the "basic beat" that is so essential to body coordination and control, and the sounds and the movements made by the children can give them the opportunity to express some of their underlying tensions and problems. When working with teen-

agers, it is a good idea to introduce this activity as a drama lesson during which they will act out various moods.

Activities to Develop Relationships

Whenever people sing together, play music together, or listen to music together, they are sharing a common experience. There are some activities that can be of special value in establishing closer relationships between the teacher and child and between the children in the group.

1. The children can bring in their favorite cassettes or recordings to which the others could listen. In a way, this is a "giving" of oneself, and any pleasure gained from the experience could lead to other ways of communicating and reaching out in a positive way.

2. Although one may not agree that music should have lyrics to be therapeutic, the suggestion that lyrics of songs deal with "love, loyalty and unity" is a valuable one. This is because part of the power of music to elicit moods is derived from the feelings it arouses, such as empathy and compassion, the "tender emotions" of love, lovemaking, love of children or parents, and other such relationships. You should teach songs with lyrics dealing with friendship, striving upwards, love, and unity. Such songs as "Impossible Dream," "We Shall Overcome," "Danny Boy," "This Land is Your Land," "You've Got to Have Heart," "If I Had a Hammer," "He's Got the Whole World in His Hands," "Born Free," "We Are the World," or the peace song "Last Night I Had the Strangest Dream" are examples of the type of music that can be used to elicit tender and/or positive feelings.

3. Any ensemble playing requires cooperation. Of great value here would be activities combining solo and group performances and partner activities. If real instruments are used, the activities are fine for adolescents.

Combine solo and group performances using the rhythm band: Divide the class into groups of four or five children and have each group work out a "refrain"—a set rhythmic section (each child could be playing a different rhythmic pattern to the same basic beat) which will recur after each child has had a chance to be soloist and to play alone as the others rest. In order to decide what their refrain will be and to give each one an opportunity to play alone, the group must work together cooperatively.

Have solo performances with group accompaniment: Have one child act as conductor and provide the basic beat as six to eight children (more could become unwieldy) improvise using rhythm instruments. Then the conductor selects one out of the group to be the soloist. This time, the others in the group do not rest, but instead continue to play softly as they provide a background accompaniment.

Have partners play the autoharp to accompany singing: Have one child press the bars indicated in the music score as the other child strums the instrument. Then they can change places. Or, two or three children can play on two or three autoharps, each one being assigned a different chord to be played at the appropriate time. There are, literally, thousands of songs that can be accompanied by using just two chords, and these are excellent for this activity. (See the song chart for those included in this book.)

Use several pupils to play a melody: Assign different phrases or measures of a song to several children and then have them play the tune on recorder or melody flute with each one playing his assigned measure. (Of course, it is assumed that they already know how to play the whole melody.) In order for the music to sound as it should, the players are required to share the responsibility and fun of performance. This activity is also suitable for those pupils learning to play instruments of the band and orchestra.

The same activity can also be done using melody or resonator bells. Both of these instruments are made up of a series of white and black metal bars arranged to resemble the piano keyboard. The bars of the melody bells (also called "song bells") are mounted on a frame and struck with a mallet (see Figure 2-2), and each bar has the name of its tone indicated on it:

Figure 2-2

The resonator bells (see Figure 2-3) have a sweet, delicate, chime-like quality. All of the bells can be separated from the set and distributed to the children:

Figure 2-3

Activities to Aid in Classroom Control

1. With the cooperation of school administration, it may be possible to use deprivation of music as a technique to modify behavior. Once rules are explained and understood, if a youngster becomes disruptive, it undoubtedly could be very helpful to have him wait elsewhere (under supervision) until he is ready again to participate in music activities. Or the child can be assigned to the "music corner"—a quiet area of the classroom where a record player with earphones, recordings, and music books and activities are kept. There, he can work quietly and separately until ready to return to the class.

2. You may find instead that the use of participation in *extra* music activities may be the technique that works best. For example, you can keep score of the child's positive behavior. Then, when the usually disruptive child has enough "plus" points, he can be rewarded by being allowed to select and listen to his favorite record. Other possible rewards could be being selected to play the drum, to lead the parade, or to choose the song the class will sing. Many teachers have found that the disruptive child's behavior will improve when music is used as a reward in this way.

3. Avoid touching activities when playing music games (e.g., dancing with partners, holding hands, circling) with hostile, aggressive children. This can lead to pushing, pulling, and twisted arms. Instead, have a large number of individual action songs, dramatizations, and music games so that they can use up some energy safely and creatively.

4. Sing gesture songs requiring considerable movement. Examples are:

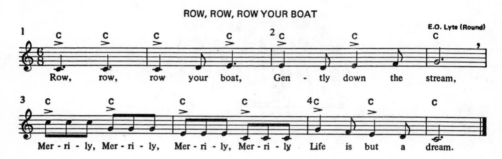

ROW, ROW, ROW YOUR BOAT

Words

Row, row, row your boat,
Gently down the stream.

Merrily, merrily, merrily, merrily,
Life is but a dream.

Motions

Rowing motions.
Waving motions of arms, moving
    left to right.

Clap hands.
Bring hands together and place
    alongside face, closing eyes.

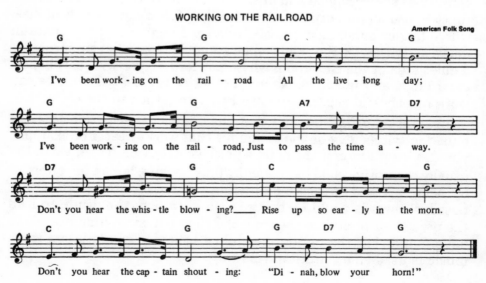

WORKING ON THE RAILROAD

(Have the pupils pretend to be laboring, building railroad tracks. They can pantomime wielding a pick-axe, digging, carrying heavy loads, etc. On, "Rise up so early in the morn," they can stretch arms up.)

There are, of course, numerous songs that can be accompanied by gestures. Some of them are useful for teaching body parts or verbs. Others can help to challenge the memory, to develop self-control, to exercise specific muscle groups, or to have the class practice following instructions. A number of these can be found in other appropriate parts of this book. (See the Correlative Song Chart for the list of these.)

5. Have the class sing "elimination" songs. Gestures are used here, but each time the song is sung, another word or group of words is eliminated until, at the end, the children are either completely or almost silent as they move. This activity has a number of values other than helping to develop a sense of rhythm. First of all, it is fun; second, the children are required to concentrate and to use self-control in order not to sing at the wrong time; finally, by the time they have finished, they are usually more relaxed. Then, after singing a more "sedative" song, they should be ready to engage in a quiet activity. A typical elimination song is "The Damper."

THE DAMPER

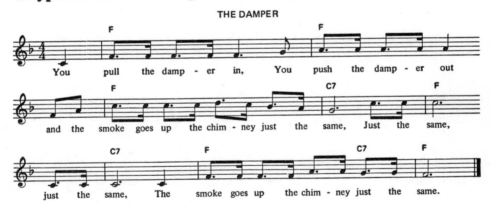

You pull the damp-er in, You push the damp-er out and the smoke goes up the chim-ney just the same, Just the same, just the same, The smoke goes up the chim-ney just the same.

Words	Motions (done only on words in italics)
You *pull* the damper in,	Draw arm towards self.
You *push* the damper out,	Push arm outwards.
And the smoke *goes up the chimney* just the same.	Wind arm upwards.
Just the same,	Stand.
Just the same,	Sit.
The smoke *goes up the chimney* just the same.	Wind arm upwards.

As in "The Damper," the song "My Hat" can be sung a number of times, keeping the gestures and eliminating additional words each time the song is sung.

MY HAT

German Folk Song

Mein Hut, er hat drei Ecke,
Drei Ecke hat mein Hut,
Und ei er hat kein Ecke,
Es sei nicht nur mein Hut.

Words	Motions
My (mein)	Point to self.
hat (Hut)	Tap head.
three (drei)	Hold up three fingers.
corners (Ecke)	Touch one elbow, then the other.
no (kein)	Shake head.
not (nicht)	Shake head.

UNDER THE SPREADING CHESTNUT TREE

Traditional

Words	Motions
Under the	Point down.
spreading	Hold arms outstretched.
chest	Point to chest.
nut	Tap head.
tree	Stretch arms overhead.
There we sat . . .	Bounce a little in seat.
just you	Point to someone else.
and me	Point to self.
Oh, how happy we would be	Clap hands.
Under the spreading . . .	Repeat motions as at start of song.

"Bingo" is also sung as an "elimination" song. Each time it is repeated, another letter is left out with the singers clapping on the beat of the omitted letter.

The "Exercise Song," done to the tune of "Yankee Doodle," can also be used in teaching parts of the body to young children. Here, too, the movements continue as more and more of the words are omitted.

6. Rules for conduct in the music class should be established and kept simple and few (i.e., Do nothing to hurt others; do nothing to hurt yourself; do nothing to hurt the instruments; do not make noises to spoil the singing or listening). Nonparticipation can be ignored and the attitude of the teacher can be, "I want you to participate. When you're ready, come back." Remember that it is very difficult for an unhappy child to sing.

7. Hyperactive children need to use up excess energy. There should be a great variety of activities—some active, some quiet—and the class should move smoothly and quickly from one to another. This means having instruments out, ready to distribute; pages marked in the song book; and record player, records, and all other materials at hand. Awkward pauses for the teacher to find the next song in the song book or to find the correct place on the record should be avoided.

8. Use special music and special chord sequences to establish classroom routines. These could include playing the same music for entering and leaving the classroom and/or starting and ending the music session with special songs. The V^7-I sequence (G^7-C; C^7-F; D^7-G on the autoharp) is a familiar pattern for such instructions as "Class, stand!" or "Sit down." The IV-I progression (F-C; C-G; B flat-F on autoharp) is the harmony used for "Amen" and is appropriate as a signal for "Let's rest" or "Quiet, please."

Others can be developed. The dominant seventh chord, for example (G^7, D^7, C^7, A^7 on the autoharp), can create a feeling of expectation and suspense. Playing it strongly several times on piano or autoharp with slight pauses between each sounding of the chord can be used to express instructions such as, "Attention, everybody," "Are you ready?" or "Please listen." The fewer words used, the better, and it is a good idea to try to use gestures and music wherever suitable.

9. Impulse control can be developed by having the pupils take turns playing a given rhythm pattern on the drum loud or soft, according to the conductor's signals. It takes special control to be able to change from loud to soft drumming at a moment's notice.

10. Sing songs that require the children to follow your instructions, and do not sing the instructions in the same order each time. (Some of these songs can be used to encourage creativity. In that case, the children would suggest the movement activities instead of

your telling them what to do.) Examples of typical "instructions" songs follow:

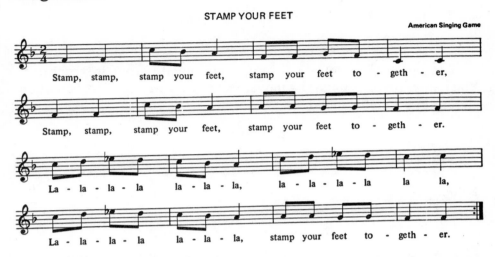

During the second half of the song, the class can continue the stamping. Or, if the children are standing in a circle, they can swing their partners or move around in a circle to the "La-la-la. . ." Other actions can be substituted for stamping feet.

Other possible movements are:

> Tap your head.
>
> Swing your arms.
>
> Snap your fingers, etc.

(This song is also useful for teaching verbs and parts of the body.)

Other possible verses are:

Now, ev'ry one tap like me.

. . ., stamp like me.

. . ., nod like me.

. . ., don't say a word.

During the last refrain, you can call out different instructions. You can gradually make the movements less and less vigorous, thus ending in a quieter mood.

MOVEMENT SONG

Here, too, sing different instructions each time. More gentle, easy-going movements would be appropriate for this song.

(Other songs that require the children to follow instructions can be found in other sections of this book. Again, see the Correlative Song Chart for a complete list of "instruction" songs in this and other chapters.)

While the music activities just described are valuable for the emotionally disturbed children, it must be remembered that *all* children can enjoy these activities and benefit from them. It is evident, also, that the teacher's response to the children is important. The stories told to the music, for example, must be accepted and the dual goals of teaching music concepts and using music to help emotions must be kept in mind. Easily obtained objectives—in music and in behavior—can help.

Working with the emotionally disturbed child in a regular classroom is, perhaps, one of the most difficult situations faced by a teacher. There is a curriculum to be taught; there are skills and understandings to be developed for all the children. But the child who is disruptive can make it difficult for the other children to learn.

Fortunately, the music activities and techniques described here can help make the situation hopeful. Music is not a panacea or a prescription for emotional ills. It *is* an excellent adjunct to all the other approaches being used with emotionally disturbed children and it can bring many moments of relief to unhappy youngsters. By incorporating more of these special activities into the school day, the teacher can help the emotionally disturbed child through some difficult times.

Happy experiences with music can lead to more and more instances of suitable behavior, socialization, and participation. In this way, all the children in the class—normal and emotionally handicapped—can benefit from the basic principles: a structured environment, as much individualization as possible, active participation, and acceptance of the child, if not of his behavior.

SUMMARY

Numerous studies have demonstrated that music activities or using music as a reward can help the emotionally disturbed child.

Self-esteem can be enhanced through achievement in learning to play an instrument or helping others play. Sometimes, simplifying or preparing special arrangements of the music is needed. Music games using the pupil's name in a positive way are also of value as are special activities in which the child has an important role to play, such as being the conductor or soloist in rhythm instrument improvisations.

Strong movements, "acting" to music, vigorous gesture songs, and songs with lively refrains can help to overcome tension, while quiet background music and "sedative" songs can enhance relaxation once tensions are released.

To encourage creativity and communication, the class can draw, write, paint, or tell stories about the music, or they can dramatize the way the music makes them feel. Any time people perform music together, they must cooperate and here, too, numerous activities can aid in developing relationships. For example, children can work together in playing autoharp accompaniments or share the playing of a melody on classroom instruments. Some songs have texts that encourage the tender emotions of gentleness, compassion, consideration, friendship, and love.

In addition, using music as a reward for good behavior or deprivation of music for misbehavior can aid in classroom control. Some songs and music activities have the intrinsic value of using up excess energy or of practicing control in cases of hyperactivity. Others add an atmosphere of fun or provide practice in following instructions.

NOTES

[1]Richard M. Graham. "Seven Million Plus Need Special Attention; Who Are They? in *Music in Special Education*. Washington, DC: Music Educators Conference, 1972. p. 23.

[2]George Giacobbe and Richard Graham. "The Responses of Aggressive Emotionally Disturbed and Normal Boys to Selected Music Stimuli." *Journal of Music Therapy*, 15, No. 3 (Fall, 1978), pp. 118–135.

[3]Norma Wasserman. "Music Therapy for the Emotionally Disturbed in a Private Hospital." *Journal of Music Therapy*, 19, No. 2 (Summer, 1972), pp. 99–104.

[4]Lee N. Baumel. "Psychiatrist as Therapist." *Journal of Music Therapy*, 10, No. 2 (Summer, 1973), p. 8.

[5]Stephen M. Henderson. "Effects of a Music Therapy Program Upon Awareness of Mood in Music, Group Cohesion, and Self-Esteem Among Hospitalized Adolescent Patients." *Journal of Music Therapy*, 20, No. 1 (Spring, 1983), pp. 14–20.

[6]Maxie C. Maultsby. "Combining Music Therapy and Rational Behavior Therapy." *Journal of Music Therapy*, 14, No. 2 (Summer, 1977), p. 93.

[7]Dorothy Brin Crocker. "Music as a Therapeutic Experience for the Emotionally Disturbed Child," *Music Therapy*. Lawrence, Kansas: Allen Press, 1958, p. 118.

[8]Juliette Alvin. *Music for the Handicapped Child*, Second Edition. London: Oxford University Press, 1976, p. 98.

[9]Suzanne Hanser. "Group-Contingent Music Listening With Emotionally Disturbed Boys." *Journal of Music Therapy*, 11, No. 4 (Winter, 1974), pp. 220–225.

[10]Carlo Ritsch. "Group Time-Out from Rock and Roll Music and Out of Seat Behavior of Handicapped Children While Riding in a School Bus." *Psychological Reports*, 31, 1972, pp. 967–973.

[11]Ronald Price, et al. "The Emotionally Disturbed Child; Out of Pandemonium, Music!" in *Music in Special Education*, pp. 19–20.

[12]Thomas J. Scott. "The Use of Music to Reduce Hyperactivity in Children." *American Journal of Orthopsychiatry*, 40, No. 4, 1970, pp. 677–680.

[13]Charles Hope Patterson, Jr. "An Experimental Study of the Effect of Soothing Background Music and Observed Behavior Indicat-

ing Tension of Third Grade Pupils" (unpublished doctoral dissertation, University of Virginia, 1959). *Dissertation Abstracts*, 20, No. 4, pp. 1271–1272.

[14]Cornell Lane. "The Effects of Three Types of Background Music on Selected Behaviors in an Elementary School Setting" (unpublished doctoral dissertation, University of Tennessee, 1976).

[15]Geralyn M. Presti. "A Levels System Approach to Music Therapy with Severely Behaviorally Handicapped Children in the Public School System." *Journal of Music Therapy*, 21, No. 3 (Fall, 1984), pp. 117–125.

[16]Catherine Windwer. "An Ascending Music Stimulus Program with Hyperactive Children." *Journal of Research in Music Education*, 29, No. 3 (Fall, 1981), pp. 173–182.

[17]Claire V. Wilson. "The Use of Rock Music as a Reward in Behavior Therapy with Children." *Journal of Music Therapy*, 13, No. 1 (Spring, 1976), pp. 39–48.

CHAPTER ✖ 3

MUSIC FOR THE
LEARNING DISABLED CHILD

According to various estimates, anywhere from one to five percent of children in the United States are learning disabled. This means that in spite of the fact that they may possess normal or above normal intelligence, they are performing below their grade level by one or more years. These children have a "disorder in one or more of the basic psychological processes involved in understanding or using language, spoken or written, which may manifest itself in an imperfect ability to listen, think, speak, read, write, spell, or do mathematical calculations."[1]

Simply stated, the learning disabled child does not achieve his or her I.Q. potential. This is not due to sensory loss, for learning disabled children hear and see. Nor are they necessarily educationally or culturally deprived; indeed, many come from homes with every advantage. They may or may not be emotionally disturbed. Some may evidence memory deficiencies or may delay response to instructions. Some are hyperactive or impulsive, but then, this can be true of normal children. In other cases, they may have difficulty forming relationships, but this can be due to their feeling different as a result of falling behind in school work. While a learning disability can be due to a brain injury, the fact that many children can outgrow their handicap or respond to the optimum type of education shows that not all learning disabled children are brain injured.

Learning disabled children can display any one or more of the following symptoms: dyslexia (difficulty in reading), perceptual-motor problems resulting in poor hand–eye coordination, aphasia (lack of speech), clumsiness, or defects in the integration of the visual and

42

auditory senses. Many have "figure-ground" problems—that is, trouble distinguishing the important from the unimportant or from understanding exactly which of the stimuli presented they are supposed to respond to.

According to Alan Ross, the eminent authority on learning disabilities, one of the factors present in most learning disabled children, whatever symptom is manifested, is a problem with "selective attention."[2] Either the child pays attention to one stimulus to the exclusion of others and that stimulus happens to be the wrong one (for example, the teacher is pointing to an arithmetic problem on the chalkboard but the child is fascinated with her pretty rings and watch), or the child's attention is divided among so many stimuli that he does not sufficiently attend to the work to be learned.

Selective attention is necessary for learning, and this is what many learning disabled children frequently need help with. Without it, hyperactivity, restlessness, school phobias, jealousies, aggressiveness, distractibility, and inability to learn can result.

Studies show that the selective attention of some learning disabled children is like that of younger normal children. Sometimes this is because of a developmental lag and the disability is eventually outgrown. Frequently, the child can be helped with training. Therefore, it is the task of the teacher and parents to aid in overcoming the disability before concomitant emotional problems result and before learning achievement falls so far behind that it is hard for the child to catch up to his or her normal grade level.

HOW MUSIC CAN HELP THE LEARNING DISABLED

What are the capabilities of the learning disabled child to learn music? Are there any specific activities or materials the music or classroom teacher can use to help alleviate some of the difficulties experienced by children with this handicap?

First of all, music ability is not related to learning disability. It is possible for a learning disabled child to be very musical, average, or below average. Usually, except for those who have difficulty remembering the sequence of words in a song, there is no problem with singing. Where there is difficulty in performing or imitating rhythms, the problem could be due to a lack of attention, poor memory, lack of interest, lack of training, or basic lack of music ability. Learning disabled children five to nine years of age generally scored lower than normal children in tests involving playing rhythm instruments with both hands, playing rhythms rapidly, hand–eye coordination, stretching their arms to play rhythm patterns, and a combination of these skills. With training and maturation, however, their scores on the compound skills test have often equalled or sometimes surpassed those of normal children.[3]

A weakness that many learning disabled children have which could affect musical performance is confusion when trying to attend to information delivered to one ear through earphones while other sounds are heard with the other ear (dichotic listening). This too has been helped with training and maturation.

Usually, learning disabled and normal children can tell whether simple rhythmic patterns they hear are the same or different. The learning disabled, however, do have trouble more often *performing* rhythmic patterns, especially the more difficult ones.[4]

In addition to the fact that musical performance of the learning disabled can be improved with training, studies have found that music activities can be an aid in improving auditory skills and in increasing retention of other aspects of the school curriculum. For example, when a combination of language development activities and music therapy was used with learning disabled children, they improved more in auditory memory and in sequencing than when only the language development activities were used.[5] And melodic-rhythmic mnemonics used as an aid in teaching multiplication tables to learning disabled children led to better results than when the tables were taught using traditional methods.[6] The findings were similar when lists of words were presented to learning disabled children—some spoken, some sung, some spoken with pictures as visual aids, and some using visuals plus singing. The children best remembered the lists of words they heard with a combination of stimuli—singing plus visuals, or visuals plus the spoken word.[7]

MUSIC ACTIVITIES

Before deciding which music activities might be of special value, you need information from resource personnel (a special education coordinator or school psychologist) clarifying the specific problem the child has. Then, activities and materials can be adapted to meet the specific symptoms.

In general, it is best to use a multi-sense approach and many modes of teaching. The learning disabled youngster may have strength in one area (e.g., motor coordination) and weakness in another (e.g., auditory perception); you should teach to the strength. For aural learners, use spoken instructions. For visual learners, add gestures.

Because a lack of selective attention is a frequent problem, stimuli should be simplified and limited to the material to be learned. In addition, provide rewards. Studies show that these can serve as motivation for the child to concentrate on the work being taught. Always use a step-by-step procedure in teaching one thing at a time.

Depending on the problem, a learning disabled child may have difficulty in motor coordination or in recognizing numbers, letters, or sounds. In music, this can result in trouble when he or she tries to read or remember music or to coordinate two hands.

Whether you are a classroom teacher with minimal music background or an experienced, competent music teacher, you can borrow some of the techniques that are used by special educators to help learning disabled children achieve in music so that they can have all its benefits and joys.

Some of the activities described here are intended to alleviate specific music performance difficulties. Others show how, by combining music with other modes of teaching, they can help the child to learn classroom work better.

Activities to Improve Motor Coordination in Performing Music

Playing two rhythms together. Go through these steps. Have the child figure out the first rhythm and then clap and count it. Have him tap the rhythm with one hand. Now do the same for the second rhythm, tapping with the other hand. Repeat the tapping of each rhythm. Practice until each step is done well. Finally, using mallets or drum sticks, play the two rhythms together on instruments.

Playing the piano with two hands together. Follow the previous procedure. After tapping the rhythm with each hand separately and then with two hands together, play them silently on a table or on the piano lid, using the correct fingering but not worrying about which keys to depress. Now do the same thing on the keyboard. The last step is to play the rhythm on the correct keys.

Crossing the body midline. Use a xylophone or similar type instrument—for example, resonator bells or two melody bells placed alongside each other. Have the child improvise a tune on the black bars, ending on the bar marked F sharp. The sound will be pleasant and the child will be moving his arm freely as he reaches from one bar to another. Repeat, using the other hand to hold the mallet.

Helping the "arrhythmic" child. For the child who can hear differences in rhythms but has trouble keeping in time and/or performing them, the activities given here can be helpful. They are also fine for developing the sense of rhythm in all children. The basic principle is to get the child moving in time to music. This is done by literally moving him (using game-like activities) so that he can actually *feel* what it is like to keep in time to a beat.

Swing Your Arms with a Partner

Children take their partners' hands and swing their arms in time to the drumbeat. An arrhythmic child, paired with a child who has a strong sense of rhythm, will find himself moved along by the partner and will begin to get the feel of moving to the music.

Play Push-and-Pull

Children take their partners' hands and, as the drum beats, they move their arms alternately in a push-pull movement, extending first one arm and then the other.

Ring the Bells

The children take their partners' hands and, as the drum beats slowly, they pretend to be ringing huge bells, swaying to the rhythm of the drum.

Play Seesaw

The children take their partners' hands and then play seesaw to the beat of the drum or to the chant: "Seesaw/Margery Daw/Johnny shall have a new master/He shall get but a penny a day/Because he can't work any faster."

As one child bends his knees to go down, the other one stands. Then they switch positions. (See Figure 3-1.)

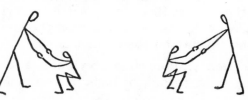

Figure 3-1

Lessening Clumsiness. Do "mirror" exercises. The easygoing pace of these activities helps to develop body control. The music can add pleasure and motivation as the pupils are required to concentrate and use selective attention as they develop a better idea of what they are doing with each body part. These activities are excellent for all grades and ages.

Mirror the Teacher

Use a recording with a moderately slow, steady dance rhythm. (Some Greek dances, like the "Hosopikos," or a slow Latin-American rumba are fine for this.) Stand in front of the room and slowly and gently, in time to the music, do "exercises"—moving your arms and shoulders, stepping forward and back, swaying, raising a leg, etc. The children, who are facing you, imitate you—for example, swaying to the left when you're moving to the right—as if they were your "mirrors."

Watch Yourself in a Mirror

Have the children do a set series of movements to music as they watch themselves in a mirror. Concentrating on their appearance will aid in developing control.

Activities to Improve Hand–Eye Coordination in Performing Music

A learning disabled child may be very musical but still have trouble reading and performing music. Robert, for example, had a remarkable music memory and "ear." At eighteen months old, he could echo melodic phrases and at five years of age, he was able to play little tunes on the piano by ear, accompanying himself with simple chords. When he eagerly started taking piano lessons at six years, they turned into a disaster. An extremely bright child, he grasped the concepts of pitch and rhythm notation immediately, but when he tried to play what he saw and understood so well, his hands and fingers would not cooperate. After months of trying, the piano lessons were stopped. Some years later, when he was an adolescent, he studied the guitar. Fortunately, this time his music teacher understood what his capabilities were. While Robert practiced reading simple guitar melodies, he learned many lovely, advanced works by rote. This enabled him to derive much pleasure from the instrument.

For a learning disabled child with a hand–eye coordination problem such as Robert's, it may be necessary to adapt the music materials so that he will find it simpler to perform what he sees and understands on the page. Some of the steps that may be taken are as follows:

Simplify the music score: Use music that has a minimal amount of material on the page—no pictures or extra words—so as not to distract the child's attention.

Use a music partner: As the child plays, you, or another child, can point to the place on the score so that he knows what he is to play next. "Losing one's place" can be a frequent difficulty until the music becomes familiar.

Write the notes in color: If the child has to play one of the parts in a musical score, go over his part with a colored pencil. That way, he won't be confused by all of the other notes on the page and will know which ones he is to play.

Use enlarged staffs: When the class is learning to play simple classroom instruments, copy the music of a child with hand–eye coordination problems onto an enlarged staff. In this way, there will be less likelihood of confusing the notes, and it will be much easier to see at a glance whether or not a note is on a line or in a space.

Stress the contour or shape of the melody: In addition to teaching the names of the notes on the lines and inside the spaces, stress the contour or shape of the melody and whether the notes are going up or down. Provide work sheets showing the scores of brief, simple, familiar melodies. As you sing the tunes or play them on melody bells, have the children draw contour lines to show the shape of the melody as it goes up and down in pitch.

MERRILY WE ROLL ALONG

Color the repeated pattern: Place the notation of a very familiar short song with repeated melodic patterns on a chalkboard or chart. Have the children sing the song and then color the notes of the repeated patterns with the same color. Now have the child play the tune on melody or resonator bells.

AU CLAIRE DE LA LUNE

Make frames: If more than one piece of music is on a page or if there are pictures or any other extraneous material on it, make a frame of cardboard or oaktag and block out everything except the music the child is to play.

Frame the staff: From a piece of oaktag, cut out an opening the width and height of the staff and place it on the music. Then move it so that the child will only see and concentrate on playing one staff at a time.

Activities to Lessen Perseveration

Some learning disabled children have trouble stopping the physical activity in which they are engaging. For them, the following activities are enjoyable, challenging, and helpful:

Play "Freeze": Have a group of children dance to recordings. Vary the tempo, type, and mood of the music. When the record is stopped, they are to freeze and remain in the position in which they are. Repeat this a number of times to give them the opportunity to express the various moods of the music. Also, play the music for different lengths of time so that it is always a surprise, requiring a quick response and control to stop movement.

Follow the conductor: Children enjoy practicing following a conductor's cues to start and stop signals, and it can be made into an enjoyable game. Have the class clap, be silent, chant a phrase at different dynamic levels, start and stop singing or playing rhythm instruments, etc., in accordance with your conducting signals. As they do this, they will be developing control and quicker responses, as in the above game. They will also be learning to follow visual signals.

Follow the drum: Tell the children that the drum is going to "talk" to them. When the drumbeat is fast, they are to clap fast. When the beat is slow, they are to clap slowly. If the drum stops, they stop.

Play a steady beat on the drum and have the children clap. Vary the tempo; play very slowly, at a moderate rate of speed or quickly, and stop suddenly to add the element of surprise and to keep the children's attention.

Move to various tempos: Establish a beat on the drum. Let the children move in time to the beat. Then change the tempo and have them change their movements. Do this several times. Sometimes you can stop playing and have them freeze.

Activities to Aid Visual Perception

Just as some learning disabled children have problems in distinguishing letters and numbers (for example, confusing 9 and 6 or b, d, and p), they can also have trouble in distinguishing musical symbols. Frequently errors are made in recognizing slight differences such as ♩ and ♭ ; ♮ and ♯ ; or ▬ and ▬ (this problem can also occur in children and adults who *don't* have a learning disability!). Those who do have problems in visual perception need special help. This can be provided through multi-sense activities and mnemonic devices.

Music is especially suited to this type of teaching because learning a symbol in music does not merely mean learning a written sign. It means being able to clap, sing, hear, feel, move, and respond to the written symbol. For learning disabled children, adding aural and motor activities takes advantage of the abilities they do have, thus increasing attention and aiding learning.

Show how to distinguish symbols (whole rest ▬ and half rest ▬)*:* Ask the children which rest has more weight (value) and which one is heavier—the whole rest or the half rest. They will usually answer, "The whole rest." Show them that the whole rest "sinks" below the line because it is heavier, while the half rest can "float" above the line because it is lighter.

Now add a face under the half-note symbol. Point out that the half rest looks like a hat: ☺   Further add that the word "hat" begins with the letters "ha" and the words "half rest" begin with "ha."

Show how to distinguish between a half note and a flat: Draw a half note on a chart. Point out that when a tire goes flat, it goes down; one part is "flattened." Next to the half note, draw a flat (♭). Show how it is a note with one part flattened because the sound goes down. Demonstrate on melody bells how the pitch goes down when a flat appears before a note, and have the class sing a tone (e.g., B) and then its flat (B♭).

Demonstrate the flat by making a large half-note symbol from pipe cleaners and then flatten one part to change it into a flat sign.

Practice writing symbols: Stress the differences between ♩ and ♪; ♪ and ⅞ . As the children learn to draw the symbols, point out detailed features. Explain how the eighth note and eighth rest have "wings" that help them to go faster, and that for the eighth rest, part of the symbol—the colored-in circle—is missing to show that the sound is missing.

Trace the symbol: Have the children trace the symbols several times or make stencils of the symbol and have the children draw around them.

Use dot-to-dot drawings: Prepare work sheets with dot-to-dot drawings of the symbols being taught and have the children connect the dots (for example: 𝄞 𝄞 ♪ ♪).

Use chants when practicing writing symbols: As the children draw the symbol, they should say the steps—first *out loud* to provide auditory reinforcement and then to themselves.

A CHANT FOR THE NATURAL SYMBOL

Draw a straight line, like this: |
Now make it an "L:" L
Add a "7," and look!   ♮
It's a natur-el |

A CHANT FOR THE G CLEF

Draw a long, straight line: |
Make a backward "S": ⌇
Add the hook: 𝄞   and the circle: 𝄞
Your clef's a success!

You can develop similar chants for other symbols. Incidentally, this type of mnemonic is useful in teaching language arts symbols. The combination of visual, auditory, and motor modes of teaching focuses the child's attention to the task at hand. Once this is done, the learning disabled child—who is of normal or above normal intelligence—can find learning simpler.

Give aural instructions: Do not rely on visual instructions. If a song, for example, is on page 14 in the song book, do not just put the page number on the chalkboard but state what page the child should turn to. Sing a song, read the words of a song out loud, or play the tune on recorder or melody bells before the child tries to read the notes. In this way, you will be teaching to strengths.

Use positioning in teaching performance on an instrument: In addition to demonstrating the fingering to be used or the bars to be played in performing on an instrument, you can help the child by positioning his fingers—putting them on the right holes or helping him to swing the mallet to the correct bar.

Show the symbols in many ways and settings: Have the symbol drawn in different colors on charts or felt boards, large and small. The use of different sizes and colors helps the child to understand that the important thing is the shape and design of the symbol, not its color, size, or position on the page. In addition, using different media reawakens attention as the learning disabled child is presented with new stimuli.

Activities to Improve Auditory Perception

Some learning disabled children cannot repeat or remember a series of spoken words or, in music, a series of tones or the words of a song. Perhaps this is because of weakness in dichotic listening, present in so many of the learning disabled. Often they will be confused by the many simultaneous sounds in music and will not be able to pick out one sound in a maze of others. For these children, visual aids should be provided and motor activities used to aid learning. In addition, there are activities which, by directing the child's attention to specific sounds, can improve auditory perception.

Move to hear high and low pitch: If you can play the piano or a melody on the bells, do so; otherwise, just play any very low tones. The children should stand as the low tones are played, and then walk around, bent low towards the ground. The children should walk on tiptoes with arms held high when the music is changed to high tones. As you change back and forth from high to low tones, varying the amount of time for each, the children should respond by either bending low or walking on their toes.

Take turns moving to changing pitch: Divide the class into three groups—high, middle, and low. As the high-pitched melodies are played on the piano or melody bells, those children who are in the high group move or dance to the music. When the music is changed to a low or middle register, the children in the high group freeze (remaining in the position in which they were when the music changed), and those children who represent the register of the new music begin to move. Vary the music so that the groups take turns dancing or remaining motionless.

Move to the song: As the children sing a familiar song, have them move their bodies up and down to indicate the rise and fall of the melody. (See Figure 3-2.)

Twink-   le,   twink-   le,   lit-   tle

star . . .

Figure 3-2

Catch high and low balls: Explain to the class that ballplayers must practice in order to play well, and therefore it is necessary for them to practice in order to hear music well. In this game, they will practice "catching" musical "high and low balls." Play a low tone on the melody bells. The pupils are to reach down and clasp their hands as they would do to catch a low ball. Then play a high tone. They are to jump high to catch a fly ball. Vary the pitch of the tones played as they practice "catch the ball" at different levels.

Move your arms to the sound of the pitch: The pupils watch as you play the vertically held melody bells, raising and lowering their arms as the pitch goes up and down.

Conduct songs to show pitch direction: As you lead a song, raise and lower your hand to show the direction of the pitch notation and sound. Have the class sing a familiar song as they look at the notation, raising and lowering their hands to show the direction of the pitch.

Sing songs combining voice, body movement, and visual stimuli: Have the children move their bodies up and down to show the direction of the pitch in songs such as the following one:

SWING SONG

Ruth Zinar

Relate the sound with the appearance of the music: Cover the score of a song or of a melody with transparency film and have the child follow along with a grease pencil as the music is heard.

All of the activities given here and others similar to them are valuable techniques for developing the sense of pitch in *all* children. Furthermore, they are excellent devices for helping the learning disabled child to concentrate on one aspect of sound at a time—in this case, melodic contour and pitch.

The child with an auditory learning disability may be confused when trying to distinguish one instrument being accompanied by others. Therefore, select music in which tone quality of the instrument is clearly illustrated and show a picture of the instrument as it is heard. If children have difficulty telling the direction from which a sound is coming, you can use games such as playing a rhythmic pattern on a drum as you walk around the room and have the children, with their eyes closed, point to the direction from which the sounds are coming. Or you can station several children in different locations in the classroom and have them take turns singing snatches of melodies or playing on rhythm instruments as the others try to guess where they are.

If a child remembers intellectually the appearance and duration values of rhythmic notation and he or she understands mathematically how measures are formed but cannot reproduce the sounds of the rhythms, add words or spoken syllable mnemonics

(♩　　♩　　♩　　♫　　♫　　𝅗𝅥　　𝅗𝅥　　𝅗𝅥　　, etc.)

| walk, | walk, | walk | run-ning, running | wa--it, | wa--it, | wa--it |
| ta, | ta, | ta; | tee-tee, tee-tee; | ta--aa, | ta--aa, | ta-aa |

During "listening lessons," you cannot tell if a child is really listening or what he is listening to. He or she may be thinking about a television program, daydreaming, listening to sounds outside the classroom, or paying attention to the rhythms when the lesson is about the families of the orchestra. Therefore, you should add visuals that are appropriate to the lesson—for example, of instruments as they sound, a melodic phrase you want the children to notice or, perhaps, if they are listening to music which is telling a story, slides or drawings on transparencies or charts for illustrative purposes. This will help them direct their attention to the facet of the music being taught. Always tell them what to listen for *before* playing a recording.

Finally, use gestures, demonstrations, and visual cues when giving directions or instructions, so that the child with an auditory perception problem will be able to participate and learn as much as possible.

Activities to Improve Auditory Memory

Some learning disabled children will remember what they *read*—perhaps even be able to recall the page number and position on the page where they read it—but have trouble remembering a series of spoken words or, in music, a series of tones or the words in a song. Instead of relying on learning songs by rote from hearing them repeated a number of times, give these children copies of the words and/or music. You can also prepare charts or transparencies with the words, or draw picture "clues" on cards or charts to hold up at the right time to help them remember the sequence of words. Furthermore, you can make tape cassettes of the songs and the pieces to be learned for them to take home. In this way, they have an extra opportunity to listen to the music and it will help them to keep up with the rest of the class.

Activities to Aid in Learning Classroom Curriculum

Some children love music and will easily remember songs and music phrases but will have difficulty memorizing facts. If their intelligence is normal or above average, this could be due to a lack of interest and the resulting lack of attention. For these children, put instructions to music or present the material rhythmically. We know that nursery school children can sing the alphabet song—which is really all nonsense syllables. This can be done because of the rhythms and attractive simplicity of the music. By setting rote material to music—whether addition problems, multiplication tables, spelling words, rules of grammar, dates, etc.—you make learning more fun. By having the children see the words as they clap and play rhythm instruments at the same time, you are using a multisense approach that attracts and holds their attention.

It is easy to develop word chants to teach different aspects of the school curriculum. Many children who have difficulty remembering facts will recall almost anything that is taught rhythmically. You can use rhythm chants in just about any subject—language arts, social studies, science, mathematics. Some of the ways you can use word chants follow. To learn plurals of some words ending in "y," write the following words on the chalkboard and have the children copy them:

lady	baby
fly	navy
sky	cry
candy	caddy
derby	daddy

Then, next to each word, have the children write the plural form as they slowly chant:

(Lady)   Change the *y* to an *i*,   (Lad*i*)
                And add "es,"   (Ladi-*es*)
                And then we have some more.

Create a social science word chant: Have the class give you four or five facts about a subject they are studying in social studies. If the topic, for example, is Abraham Lincoln, the sentence might be:

Abraham Lincoln freed the slaves.

He was our sixteenth president.

He was known for his honesty.

He was assassinated.   He was assassinated.

Divide the class into four groups and assign a different sentence to each. Have each group repeat its part in rhythm (as indicated) several times and then in combination with another group. Add the sentences until all are chanted together. You can also use a different rhythm instrument (drum, tambourine, maraca, rhythm sticks) for each rhythm. The effect will be interesting and will help to reinforce the information.

To learn long and short vowels: Put on the chalkboard the symbols for long and short vowels (for example, ā, ă; ē, ĕ; ī, ĭ). Have the children chant as they write in the appropriate symbol for long or short vowels:

ă is short!
ă is short!
Short, short, short,
ă is short.
ā is long, _____
ā is long, _____
Long, _____, Long _____,
ā is long, etc.

Sing a song about long and short vowels: Put on the chalkboard the long and short vowels being studied. Make up lists of words with long and short vowels similar to the following:

ă	ā
măn	māne
căn	cāne
măt	māte
hăt	hāte
păn	pāne
văn	vāne

As you point to the symbols and the words, have the children sing to the tune of "Twinkle, Twinkle, Little Star":

> ă is short and ā is long,
> Add the "e" to make it long.
> ă for "măn" and ā for "māne,"
> ă for "căn" and ā for "cāne"
> ă is short and ā is long,
> Add the "e" to make it long.

Rote material can also be set to simple melodies. If possible, use familiar tunes so that the children don't also have to learn a new tune. If you can't think of one to fit, any repeated fragment of a melody will do. This was shown in the study by Patricia K. Shehan[8] in which she had learning disabled children memorize lists of words sung on the same two tones repeated for each word; no attempt was made to set the words to an attractive song, but the children remembered lists of words heard that way better than they did when lists of words were spoken. The important thing is to keep the rhythm going.

Sing a grammar song (to the tune of "Twinkle, Twinkle, Little Star"):

> "Go," a verb, an action word,
> Noun's a person, place or thing.
> Adjectives describe the best,
> Conjunctions add up all the rest.
> Pronouns such as "he," "she," "they,"
> End our grammar song today.

Teaching a Song to a Class That Includes Several Learning Disabled Children

Let us assume that you want to teach the children in your class the French folk song, "How Do You Plant Your Cabbages?" You want to add movement activities and classroom instruments and you want the children to suggest different ways to plant cabbages. You also wish to show them something about music reading—in this case, melodic repetition and the relationship between the sound and notation of rising and falling pitch.

Among the other children in the class are several learning disabled youngsters. Your goals for the learning disabled are twofold. First, you want them to enjoy participating with the other children in making music together; for this, you would teach to their strengths so that they have a feeling of achievement and satisfaction. Second, you want as much as possible, to alleviate their difficulties in learning and performing music, whether due to visual-perception, auditory-memory, auditory, or motor coordination problems.

There are many activities you can use which all the children will enjoy. Special materials or assignments for the learning disabled can give them the opportunity to excel in those areas in which they can, and can help to improve skills where there is a weakness.

The music on the page in the song book might look like this:

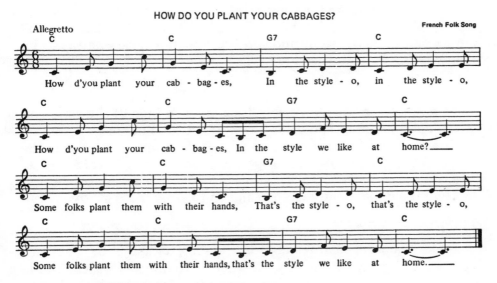

Have you ever planted cabbages?
Do you know how cabbages are really planted?
What is needed to plant seeds?

Resonator or melody bells part. (Play throughout.):

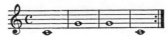

Note to the Teacher: Have the children suggest different ways to plant cabbages (e.g., with the feet, heels, nose, head, etc.). They can tap the ground with the part of the body named.

"How Do You Plant Your Cabbages?" can be used as a "name" song. Each time it is repeated, a different child's name can be used and the child can suggest how the cabbages could be planted (e.g., "How does John plant his cabbages?" or "How does Patty plant her cabbages?").

Activities for Child "A" with Auditory Perception Problems

Start with visual stimuli. Using a large chart with the melody on it, have child "A" come up to the chart and show how the notes go up and down.

Sing the song as you point to the notes going up and down.

Have the children sing the melody as they raise and lower their hands to indicate the pitch direction.

Let child "A" (a visual learner) come to the chart and find the measures in which the melody repeats.

Have the class sing the song, raising their hands when the melody repeats. As he sees the other children raise their hands, "A" will know when to do the same and will begin to associate what he hears with what he sees on the chart.

Activities for Child "B" with an Auditory Memory Problem

In addition to the above activities, make a tape of the song and let the child listen to it during "free" quiet-time periods.

Draw pictures on cards of the parts of the body mentioned in the song and hold them up at the proper times to serve as visual reminder cues.

Give the child a copy of the song to take home to study.

Activities for Child "C" with a Visual Perception Problem

Make a special, enlarged copy of the song for child "C," eliminating everything but the melody—the autoharp indications, the words of the song, tempo markings, the music for the resonator bells, the questions, the "notes to the teacher." The concept being taught here is the relationship between pitch notation and sound; therefore the score should direct the child's attention solely to this.

Present the auditory stimulus first. Sing the song several times and let child "B" (an auditory learner) demonstrate, by raising and lowering his arms, how the sound goes up and down. Now let him lead the class as they all do this while singing.

Show the music chart and have the class sing the melody with neutral syllables as they move their arms to indicate the pitch direction.

Distribute mimeographed copies of the song and have the children trace the melody as they sing the tune. Or they can draw on transparency film placed on top of the page in the music book.

Have the children suggest a different rhythm instrument for each part of the body named in the song.

Demonstrate the melody of the resonator bells part several times, explaining how it is done. Let some children with good "ears" for music and good motor coordination try to play the bells.

Distribute the rhythm instruments and let the child with a visual-perception disability play one of these (no reading ability is required for these) or else let him conduct the class as they play and sing.

Activities for Child "D" with a Motor Coordination Problem

After learning the song, let the class sing it, hitting their desks on the first beat of each measure. Go around the room, gently moving the arms of some of the children to the music. Do this with several children without motor coordination difficulties, as well as with the child who has the problem. In this way, you will not be calling attention to the disability.

Distribute instruments, giving the drum to child "D." Have the child play on the first beat, helping in the same way.

Demonstrate the resonator bells part. Have the children make believe that they are playing the bars on their desks.

Let child "D" try to play the resonator bells part.

Coordinate the activities. Have the children sing the song with gestures while some play the instruments.

Teaching a piece for recorder or melody flute to a class that includes several learning disabled children

The activities described for teaching a song can be adapted.

To improve the skills of the child with poor visual perception, make a separate, enlarged copy of the melody, omitting autoharp indications, rhythm band instrument parts, etc. Let him hear the tune several times. Also let him excel by having a chance to play a rhythm instrument part which would not require music reading skills.

For the child with poor hand–eye coordination, help him by pointing to each measure as it is reached, or by using a card to block out all but the staff being read. You can also aid him by positioning his fingers on the instrument—actually moving them for him.

Have the children go through these steps before trying to play a piece: Clap the rhythms; say the names of the notes in rhythm; move their fingers on the instruments as if playing, as you say the names of the notes; play the piece as you say the names of the notes; play the piece again as you go around the room, helping to position fingers where necessary.

Memorizing a simple autoharp accompaniment, playing a rhythm band instrument, or even playing a more difficult resonator bell part learned by ear are ways the child with hand–eye coordination problems can participate.

For the child with auditory-perception or auditory memory problems, make a tape of the music for him to listen to at home. Let him look at the music, naming the notes, before trying to play it.

By using these many modes of teaching, you will not only be able to help the learning disabled child participate and happily achieve in music, but you will be providing a good musical background and joyous experiences for all the children in your class.

SUMMARY

Children with learning disabilities have normal or above normal intelligence but may have one or more problems with visual or auditory perception, hand–eye coordination, auditory memory, or motor control. These deficits interfere with learning. Because music activities combine visual, auditory, and motor skills, they can aid in focusing the pupil's attention on the matter to be learned. Studies have shown that using rhythmic chants or songs together with movement facilitates learning various aspects of the class curriculum. The creative teacher can develop many of these music activities for subjects such as language arts and mathematics.

The learning disabled child can participate in music activities if the methods used teach to his strengths: the child with visual perception problems can be encouraged to use his auditory abilities, while the pupil with poor auditory memory can be helped by numerous visual cues and aids. Some special music activities can combat difficulties in performing that result from poor hand–eye coordination or motor control or from perseveration.

Because of the various causes and types of learning disabilities, different procedures should be developed for each child.

NOTES

[1]Federal Register, 43, no. 250. Thursday, December 29, 1977; "Section 121a.5 Handicapped Children (9)."

[2]Alan O. Ross. *Learning Disability; The Unrealized Potential.* New York: McGraw Hill, 1977, pp. 96 ff.

[3]Janet Perkins Gilbert. "A Comparison of the Motor Music Skills of Nonhandicapped and Learning Disabled Children." *Journal of Research in Music Education*, 31, No. 2 (Summer, 1983), pp. 147–155.

[4]Betty W. Atterbury. "A Comparison of Rhythm Pattern Perception and Performance in Normal and Learning Disabled Readers Age Seven and Eight." *Journal of Research in Music Education*, 31, No. 4 (Winter, 1983), pp. 259–270.

[5]Kay Lee Sherwood Roskam. "Music Therapy as an Aid in Increasing Auditory Discrimination and Improving Reading Skills." (Unpublished doctoral dissertation. University of Kansas, 1977.)

[6]Kate E. Gfeller. "Musical Mnemonics as an Aid to Retention with Normal and Learning Disabled Students." *Journal of Music Therapy*, 20, No. 4 (Winter, 1983), pp. 179–189.

[7]Patricia K. Shehan. "A Comparison of Mediation Strategies in Paired-Associate Learning for Children with Learning Disabilities." *Journal of Music Therapy*, 18, No. 3 (Fall, 1981), pp. 120–127.

[8]Ibid.

CHAPTER ✖ 4

MUSIC FOR THE TRAINABLE
MENTALLY RETARDED CHILD

The trainable mentally retarded (TMR) have I.Q.'s of about thirty-five to fifty-five. They not only have impaired intelligence, but they also function below normal in social, motor, and sensory facets of life. TMR children have trouble getting along in the outside world and throughout their lives they need support from others. Some have limited vocabularies, while others at the lower end of the intelligence scale may be nonverbal. Confusion about their body parts and about the relationship of themselves to others is frequent. They tend to be clumsy with an awkward gait and have slower motor responses than those of normal or educable retarded children. Those with lower intelligence sometimes have stereotyped movements such as uncontrolled rocking.

TMR children have poor short-term memories so that given a series of numbers, words, or pictures to learn, they tend to forget the first of the series by the time they see or hear the last. However, with training, their short-term memory is similar to that of normal children of the same mental age.[1]

Trainable mentally retarded children can have the same emotional problems as those with average intelligence, and these can result in lowered self-image, inhibitions, withdrawal, or aggressive behavior.[2] These problems result from unhappy life experiences and rejection, over-permissiveness, or neglect by parents or others. Used to failure, they tend to give up easily instead of "trying harder the next time." Yet, when given love and the opportunity to learn basic social skills and to develop to their full potential, they can be affectionate and eager for approval and can become very attached to a teacher.

They respond best when given praise, rewards, and the opportunity to achieve. When a few mentally retarded children were rewarded with praise for "paying attention" to working with manipulative toys, not only did *their* performance improve, but some of their peers who did not receive praise responded to the warmth of the overheard approval and also began to be more attentive.[3]

By and large, the trainable mentally retarded can eventually be expected to achieve through about the first- or second-grade level and to live a semi-independent life at home or in a sheltered situation.

These characteristics suggest the important role that music can play in the education of the trainable mentally retarded because of their problems in communication. For the child who has little language skills, it can enable him to express himself in a nonverbal way. Also, through the use of appropriate song material, it can help to provide a basic vocabulary. One of the most important aspects in the education of the severely retarded is the development of self-esteem. This can be enhanced not only through feelings of accomplishment in performing music but also through learning body parts from songs and music games using the child's name. In addition, in areas of caring for one's self, body control, and everyday skills and social behavior, music is an excellent resource, both as reward and teaching device.

MUSICAL CHARACTERISTICS OF THE
TRAINABLE MENTALLY RETARDED

Trainable mentally retarded children have considerably lower scores on musical aptitude and talent tests than do normal or educable retarded children of the same age. They do, however, have very much the same abilities as children of the same mental age. Thus, in general, an eleven-year-old trainable mentally retarded child with an I.Q. of forty-five could be expected to perform in music at the same level as a kindergarten child, and at sixteen, at the level of a second grader. Various studies have found characteristics that would affect how much can be accomplished with and through music.

The severely retarded can recognize differences in tempo and, indeed, where stereotypic behavior (such as rocking) exists, it can be affected by the rate of speed of the music they hear. Because it is felt that such uncontrolled movements interfere with the learning process, efforts have been made to see what kind of music could decrease the speed and frequency of rocking. While some researchers agree that faster music makes the "medium" rockers (those who rock about five times a minute) rock faster,[4] still others have concluded that stimulating music *decreases* the autisms or uncontrolled movements in severely retarded boys with I.Q.'s up to fifty-five.[5] Speeding up the same music from the correct 33 RPM to 45 RPM has led, in some cases, to even more rocking and to more uncontrolled vocalizations. But when the music was played even faster, at 78 RPM, these types of movements and vocalizations were lessened. It is not certain why the speed of the music affects stereotyped movements in what appears to be an erratic way. Perhaps when the music becomes very fast, the feeling for a strong beat is lost and therefore the movements are lessened. Apparently, it is necessary "to determine empirically the particular rate of rhythmicity that is most effective in reducing a particular form of stereotyping."[6]

When a group of trainable mentally retarded were asked to state whether one measure rhythms in $\frac{2}{4}$ meter were the same or different from each other, I.Q. was found to be the most important relationship. Thus, the scores of retardates of various ages with I.Q.'s of forty-five were more closely related to each other than those of the same age with different I.Q.'s.[7]

The severely retarded respond most to the rhythmic aspects of music but when other factors in addition to rhythmic perception are introduced, they have difficulty in distinguishing more than one aspect of music at a time.

Because of their short attention spans and easy distractibility, up to two minutes is probably as long as they can be expected to remain seated listening to music at any one time. They like to listen to vocal music more than to instrumental music, to rhythmic music more than less rhythmic, and to children's music more than to electronic or "adult" music. In general, then, their preferences are the same as those of other children of the same mental age.[8] Like most other children, they are very responsive to "live" music. They love to watch the movements of the players, and talking about and finding words to express how the music sounds to them can help them to verbalize more readily.

Motor coordination and motor responses of the trainable mentally retarded are slower than, and probably about three years behind, those of the educable mentally retarded, and they are poor at imitating clapping and in keeping time to music. They do find duple ($\frac{2}{4}$) rhythms simpler to perform than triple ($\frac{3}{4}$). They also have little singing ability until about five years of age and have lower pitched voices and a much smaller singing range (the distance from the lowest to the highest tone) than that of normal children.

With all these deficits in musical abilities, attention span, and memory, it would seem that there could be little accomplishment in music for trainable retarded children. Yet, there have been surprising results when they have been given individualized instruction in performance. According to the Baldwin Electrosystem Music Education Division,[9] trainable retarded children at several institutions (a state diagnostic clinic for the developmentally disabled, a school hospital for the mentally retarded, and a county school) were taught to play keyboard music in electronic laboratories. The pupils all had their own keyboards with earphones, enabling the music teacher to give them individualized instruction, and they were able to learn to play simple keyboard music.

In another study, several hundred eight to sixteen year olds with I.Q.'s of less than fifty participated in vocal and instrumental activities in a special program in a Philadelphia district.[10] They had many success experiences resulting in enhanced self-image and were eventually able to participate in instrumental ensembles by playing very simple parts on cue from the conductor.

Through repeated drills and exercises, a small group of students, ten to twenty-one years old with Down's Syndrome, were taught by rote to play simple melodies on clarinet, alto saxophone, flute, and cornet. Eventually, they learned to play 38 songs, and performed at a Music Educators National Conference meeting and on a national network television program. So highly motivated were they to learn to play, that there was no problem with attention and their private lessons lasted up to two-and-a-half hours![11]

This motivation to learn and to participate in music activities is further demonstrated by the experiences of the eminent music therapists Paul Nordoff and Clive Robbins who found the severely retarded eager to participate in musical productions and ready to rehearse for long periods at a time to learn their parts.[12]

Music used as a reward has also motivated the trainable retarded. In one study, when a TMR child was able to imitate a music behavior correctly (for example, clap hands three times, stamp feet four times, ring the bells, and play three or more consecutive tones on the xylophone) he would be rewarded by a music listening interval.[13] As a control, either there would be no reward or else the music was played whether or not the imitation was correct. When music was played whether or not the child performed accurately, there was little improvement in responses. However, when the music listening was used as a reward for correct imitation, there was a substantial increase in accuracy. Music listening used as a reward has also helped to decrease stereotyped movements.[14]

It is not only through private or individualized instruction or through the use of music as a reward that the trainable mentally retarded benefit from music activities. Those who participated in a choir made significantly fewer errors in auditory discrimination than their peers who were not choir members.[15] And when some one hundred pupils with average I.Q.'s of forty-seven were taught using two learning situations, one with stories and one with songs, they remembered a larger number of items from the song situation.[16]

Music has also been used to teach severely retarded children to write.[17] At first, gross body and arm movements in time to music were used, and these were gradually refined until finger motion was controlled, with the pupils finally writing exercises on the chalkboard in time to music.

Apparently, in spite of the fact that their musical abilities are so much lower than those of other children of the same chronological age, the severely retarded enjoy music and can learn. Many teachers agree that "once . . . [they] learn a song, they never seem to forget it!"[18]

MUSIC ACTIVITIES

Classroom music activities for the retarded child include many that every child (whether slow, average, or bright) can enjoy. Some are adapted to make learning simpler; some are suitable for any child who has not yet learned them. *All* children learn music better if a multi-sense approach is used, including activities for body, eye, ear, and voice, and if all facts are demonstrated by concrete representations. This is especially true of the retarded. The activities for the trainable mentally retarded that are suggested here are of two types: those that they can usually accomplish and those that can help them in learning basic life skills.

The physical, intellectual, and social characteristics and needs of retarded children suggest a number of attitudes and approaches that can be most helpful. In music, as in other areas, much encouragement is needed. Instead of making a challenging statement such as "This is hard," or "See if you can do it," give them something to do in which they can anticipate success. Statements like, "You can do this well," and "I know you can," are what they need; and when they do learn something new, they should receive warm praise and approval.

While every child should be helped to progress as much as possible, competition should be avoided in music instruction for the retarded. The Suzuki violin method is an excellent illustration of this. All the children taught using this method are praised any time they learn something well. At a Suzuki recital, you will find the most advanced pupils playing difficult compositions. Then, as the performance continues and the difficulty of the pieces decreases, more and more of the children join in until at the end, all of them are playing a simple melody together. The whole class is greeted with warm applause; everyone is accepted for what he can do.

Introduce new tasks one at a time and break up learning into the smallest possible progressive steps. For example, to learn to clap a rhythm pattern, they would first have to be able to clap a simple beat.

For children who have difficulty understanding what they hear, always use gesture, pictures, visual aids, or movement and keep instructions clear and brief, giving one at a time.

Try to follow the same routines and structure in a lesson. In my own teaching experience, I departed from this on one occasion and instead of starting the music class with the same few familiar songs sung in the same order, I tried a different song and omitted one of the usual ones. The result was restlessness and a vague feeling of unhappiness among the children. Even starting a song with a slightly different introduction can result in confusion. Once, a trainable mentally retarded child with an extraordinary ear for music noticed when a song was played in a different key and insisted that it was wrong!

Frequent repetitions of songs and instrumental material may be required for the mentally handicapped. But don't make the mistake of overpracticing to achieve perfection. Indeed, it is not perfection but enjoyment for which you should strive.

Because of these children's short attention spans, plan for a number of different activities and/or scatter music activities throughout the day. If you remember that the musical ability of the trainable retarded is correlated with mental age rather than with chronological age and that the older trainable retardate with an I.Q. of c. forty-five can probably eventually learn as much as a second-grader, it will be easier to plan activities.

Singing Activities

1. Select songs that are meaningful to the children. Where there are new words to be learned, they should, as much as possible, be those that can be explained by actions or gestures suggested by the song, or taken from the child's environment, or illustrated by concrete representations.

2. In selecting songs for the trainable mentally retarded, choose short ones of about a minute in length and those which have a limited vocal range. (See Chapter 5 on music for the educable retarded for examples of songs with limited singing range.) If possible, keep the melody within the following tone limits—lower than those for the average child:

3. If possible, include songs that have universal appeal so that the trainable mentally retarded can have the pleasureable experience of singing together with others. You don't have to feel that you must teach only nursery or preschool rhymes.

If you study many of the available school song books intended for different grades, you will often find many of the same songs included in them. This is not an error. Many songs are suitable for many age groups and these are the ones best for a mainstreamed class. After all, a folk song is one which has proven itself to have universal appeal. Many collections for kindergarten, first, and second grade will include folk songs enjoyed by children of the same chronological age as well as by people of all ages. A glance at the titles in these books shows such songs as "Bingo," "Frère Jacques," "Hokey Pokey," "Hush Little Baby," "Old McDonald," "Michael, Row the Boat Ashore," "There's a Little Wheel," "Kum-Ba-Yah," "Battle Hymn of the Republic" (the refrain), and "If You're Happy," all of which have repetitious words and/or simple melodic patterns.

4. It has been found that the best results for eliciting a singing response occur when trainable mentally retarded children are accompanied by a solo singing voice.[19] More join in the attempt to sing than when they are accompanied by piano, guitar, or a group of singers. Some severely retarded children respond best with guitar or piano and therefore, if possible, they should also be used. But the teacher who cannot play an instrument need not feel discouraged;

his or her own singing together with the children would be the most favorable way of having the greatest amount of participation.

5. Trainable mentally retarded children are not able to sing rapidly, and songs normally sung at a moderately quick pace have to be sung more slowly with them.

6. Songs with repeated melodic patterns or refrains are enjoyed. Variety in the singing can be introduced by the method of singing the refrain—loud or soft, with actions or rhythm instruments.

7. As indicated by their need for routine, have a few familiar songs with which you can start music activities, and it is a good idea to have the children sing them in the same order each time.

8. Use songs to expand the children's vocabularies, teaching colors, concepts of "up and down," "high and low," "left and right," and "fast and slow," names of the children, social behaviors, etc. Wherever necessary, provide pictures or gestures as cues to the meanings of the new words. Because of the trainable retardate's impaired self-image, many body parts songs and those which require actions based on the words of the songs are especially valuable.

Examples of such songs follow:

Other possible verses are:

Stamp your feet;   Turn around;
Nod your head;   Touch your nose;
Shake your hips;   Close your eyes, etc.

NOTE: This version of "If You're Happy" has been pitched lower and the rhythm simplified for trainable mentally retarded children.

This song ("If You're Happy") can have a number of applications in teaching. In addition to learning body parts and verbs, the children follow instructions. If they can suggest something new for each verse, creativity is being encouraged, motor coordination is aided, and tensions are released. In addition, if they try to remember any of the previously sung verses and repeat them each time, it becomes an exercise in memory as they sing a "cumulative" song.

IF YOU CLAP YOUR HANDS

Song Game
(based on French Folk Song)

If you clap your hands, then we'll clap hands just like you.__ If you clap your hands, then we'll clap hands just the same. Just the same, just the same, clap hands just the same.

Other possible verses:

If you stamp your feet; swing your arms; tap your head, etc.

(Other concepts can be introduced in some verses: for example, If you sing so soft; If you sing out loud; If you stand up tall; If you wash your face; If you say "Hello"; If you shake my hand.)

Some "direction" songs (left and right, up and down, high and low) are:

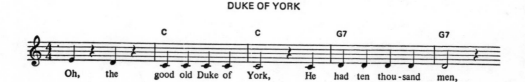

DUKE OF YORK

Oh, the good old Duke of York, He had ten thou-sand men,

He marched them up to the top of the hill and he marched them down a-gain. And when they were up they were up, And when they were down they were down, And when they were on-ly half way up, they were nei-ther up nor down.

Words	Motions
He marched them up. . . .	Stand up.
He marched them down again.	Sit down.
And when they were up they were up	Stand up.
When they were down. . . .	Sit.
When they were half way up	Stand in crouching position.
They were neither up nor down.	Stretch high, standing on tiptoes and then sit down.

Have the children pretend to be hitting a drum with the indicated hand:

PLAYING THE DRUM

R.Z.

Right! Right! Play the drum! Right! Right! With a rum - tum - tum!

Left! Left! With left hand! Left! Left! In the big brass band!

CIRCLE TO THE LEFT

The following song is helpful in teaching verbs, body parts, and the concepts of "left" and "right." It can also be used to practice following instructions. The motions are indicated by the words of the song:

OLD RED WAGON

2. Circle to the right, old red wagon . . .
3. Shake your right hand now, old red wagon . . .
4. Shake your left hand now . . .
5. Stamp your left foot now, old red wagon . . .
6. Stamp your right foot . . .
7. Wiggle left hip now . . .
8. Ev'rybody in . . .
9. Ev'rybody out . . .

"Hokey-Pokey" also deals with left and right and parts of the body. (When danced to a syncopated beat, it has been enjoyed by teenagers and adults):

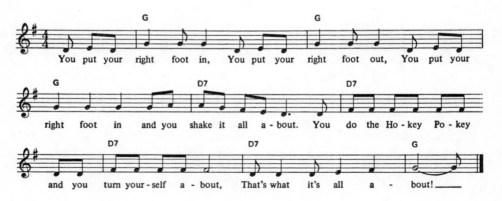

HOKEY POKEY

Other verses:

You put your left foot in (right arm, left arm, left hip, right hip,
right shoulder, left shoulder, whole self, etc.)

GO IN AND OUT THE WINDOW

Go in and out the win-dow, Go in and out the win-dow,

Go in and out the win-dow, As we have done be-fore.

Other verses can be:

Go round and round the circle; Go stand behind the table;
Go crawl beneath the table; Go shake hands with your partner, etc.

The "Swinging Song" found in Chapter 3 can also be used in
teaching up and down and high and low.

The "name songs" in Chapter 2—"What is Billy Wearing" and
"Won't You Sit Down"—are also of value in teaching the different
colors. The melody for "What is Billy Wearing" may be too difficult
for trainable retarded children and "Won't You Sit Down" requires
some rhyming ability. They are, however, suitable for the teacher to
sing for the children.

Playing Musical Instruments with the
Trainable Mentally Retarded

Obviously, the classroom teacher, the special education teacher, or
even the school music teacher will not, under most conditions, be
able to give private instruction for playing instruments to the severely retarded in their classes. This has been accomplished only under
special optimum circumstances. But the fact that some trainable
retarded have been able to learn how to play keyboard and band instruments demonstrates that they can enjoy participating in using
those instruments found in the usual classroom situations.

PLAYING THE AUTOHARP

The autoharp is a very simple instrument to play. It is done by simultaneously pressing a button indicating the name of the desired chord and strumming the strings. Most children enjoy having a chance to play accompaniments for songs and/or melody instruments, and it can be an excellent opportunity for you to give the trainable retarded child a chance to participate in a classroom orchestra.

There are many songs for which the harmonies can be simplified so that they can be accompanied by playing just one chord repeatedly—the easiest type of accompaniment. If one child holds the button down while another does the strumming, it can be made even simpler. If a song is too long—and if it can be harmonized by playing only one chord—the child can participate by accompanying the singing.

Among the songs that can be harmonized in this way are:

MY GOOSE

SWING LOW, SWEET CHARIOT

Verse 2: If you get there before I do,
Coming for to carry me home,
Just tell my friends I'm coming too,
Coming for to carry me home.

THERE'S A HOLE IN THE BUCKET

(The boys sing Georgie's part; the girls sing Liza's.)

American Folk Song

Georgie: There's a hole in the buck - et, dear Li - za, dear Li - za, There's a
Liza: Then why don't you mend it, dear Geor - gie, dear Geor - gie, Then

hole in the buck - et, dear Li - za, a ___ hole!
why don't you mend it, dear Geor - gie, mend the hole!

Verse 2: Georgie: With what should I mend it dear Liza, dear Liza,
With what should I mend it, dear Liza, with what?
Liza: With a straw you should mend it, dear Georgie,
dear Georgie,
With a straw you should mend it, dear Georgie,
with a straw.

Verse 3: Georgie: But the straw is too long, dear Liza,
dear Liza. . . .
Liza: Then why don't you cut it, dear Georgie,
dear Georgie. . . .

Verse 4: Georgie: With what should I cut it, dear Liza. . . .
Liza: With a knife, you should cut it, dear Georgie. . . .

Verse 5: Georgie: But the knife is too dull. . . .
Liza: Then why don't you hone it. . . .

Verse 6: Georgie: With what should I hone it. . . .
Liza: With a stone you should hone it. . . .

Verse 7: Georgie: But the stone is too dry. . . .
Liza: Then why don't you wet it. . . .

Verse 8: Georgie: With what should I wet it. . . .
Liza: With water you wet it. . . .

Verse 9: Georgie: With what should I fetch it. . . .
Liza: With a bucket you fetch it. . . .

Verse 10: Georgie: But there's a hole in the bucket, dear Liza. . . .

FRÈRE JACQUES

French Folk Song

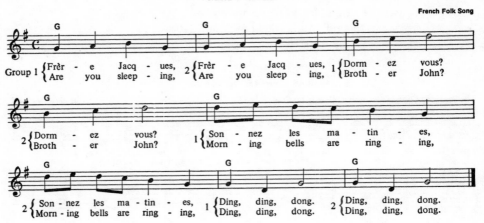

Group 1 {Frèr - e Jacq - ues, 2{Frèr - e Jacq - ues, 1{Dorm - ez vous?
{Are you sleep - ing, {Are you sleep - ing, {Broth - er John?

2{Dorm - ez vous? 1{Son - nez les ma - tin - es,
{Broth - er John? {Morn - ing bells are ring - ing,

2{Son - nez les ma - tin - es, 1{Ding, ding, dong. 2{Ding, ding, dong.
{Morn - ing bells are ring - ing, {Ding, ding, dong. {Ding, ding, dong.

LIZA JANE

American Folk Tune

I've got a gal and you've got none, L'il Li - za Jane,

I've got a gal and you've got none, L'il Li - za Jane.

Refrain:
Oh, E - li - za, l'il Li - za Jane, Oh, E - li - za, l'il Li - za Jane.

Verse 2: Got a house in Baltimore,
Li'l Liza Jane,
Lots of children 'round the door,
Li'l Liza Jane.

LITTLE TOMMY TINKER

Round Traditional

Lit - tle Tom-my Tin - ker, sat on a clin - ker, and he be - gan to cry,

Ma,_____ Ma,_____ poor lit - tle in - no - cent guy.

SHALOM CHAVERIM

LITTLE DAVID

Verse 2: Joshua was the son of Nun,
He never would quit
'til his work was done.

Verse 3: I told you once, I told you twice,
You can't get to heaven by
shooting dice.

Additional one-chord songs are listed on the Correlative Song Chart, beginning on page xi.

PLAYING A CLASSROOM WIND INSTRUMENT

The recorder, popular during the fifteenth through eighteenth centuries, has a lovely, sweet tone and is often taught to elementary school children. There are, however, certain difficulties inherent in learning the instrument. Careful breath control is needed or it will "overblow" (play an octave—eight notes—higher) or squeak. Fingers must be firmly and carefully placed on the correct holes to prevent air from escaping from the wrong ones. The fingering for some of the tones is a little complicated, using combinations of fingers that may require fine coordination in addition to remembering how to play the tones. This may be troublesome for some pupils.

For those children who might have a problem with breath control, finger control, or remembering the fingering, some simple classroom wind instruments—including tonette, song flute, and flutophone—have been developed. On these instruments, the finger holes are raised and thus are more easily felt. Some of the instruments even have thumb rests on their backs to make them easier to hold. Smaller in size and with the finger holes closer together, they are suitable for small hands. The most important benefits of all though for teaching the mentally retarded are that fingering is much simpler and it would take extremely enthusiastic blowing to result in squeaking.

The best classroom wind instrument for older trainable retarded children (those with a mental age of seven years) would be a tonette or melody flute because of the simple fingering and because they can learn to play simple three- and, perhaps, four-tone melodies. Instead of teaching them music notation, use a rote approach. Fingering for one note at a time should be taught and perfected before you go on to the next one. When they know where to put their fingers for the tones "G" and "A," you can have them play two-tone melodies by calling out the names of the notes. Later, they can read the letter symbols for these notes from large charts as they play. When that is accomplished, the fingering for "B" can be added, etc.

Sometimes, children's lack of ability precludes them from this activity. In ensemble playing where they will participate with other children, as those who have learned to read music or to play several tones on recorder, melody flute, or song bells perform their parts, those children unable to do more than blow into an instrument can play a "prepared" tonette or melody flute on cue. If, for example, the only note needed for an accompaniment is a repeated "B," you can cover with adhesive cloth the holes for the thumb and index finger of the left hand. By doing this the child will just have to blow into the instrument on time. If "G" is needed, all the upper holes played by the left hand can be covered with tape.

Another useful wind instrument for the severely retarded is the kazoo. Here, no special fingering is needed as they just "toot" the melody into the instrument; this can also be of help in having the child find his singing voice. Or you can use single-tone reed horns, with each child playing his own different tone on his own horn on cue to form a melody.

PLAYING RHYTHM INSTRUMENTS

Because of their poor motor coordination, the trainable mentally retarded can best participate in a rhythm band by playing on the basic beat. Not all instruments are equally suitable for this. The triangle would present difficulties because of its tendency to swing and change position as it is struck and also because the slender metal beater requires fine motor control to be held properly. The tone block also calls for more coordination ability than instruments like bongo drums, maracas, tambourine or "jingle" bells. Where a child has trouble grasping a drumstick, he can be helped if you wrap tape around the stick to "fatten" it.

Some children may never be able to pass the stage of sitting on the floor and beating a drum as you hold it for them. Others who are more capable may be able to play creative and interesting rhythms, while still others can learn short, repetitive rhythm patterns in $\frac{2}{4}$ and $\frac{4}{4}$ meter. When playing freely on a drum or rhythm instrument, most trainable retarded children will be able to think in terms of playing fast or slow or loud or soft; trying consciously to combine two ways of playing (for example, "soft and fast," "loud and fast," "slow and loud," "slow and soft") would be too difficult for them.

PLAYING RESONATOR BELLS

Unlike the piano keyboard, each bar of the resonator bells set has the name of its tone on it so that you do not have to be familiar with a keyboard in order to be able to play the correct bars. In addition, all of the bells can be separated from the set and distributed to the children. Thus, depending on their abilities, a melody can be played by one, two, or more children. For the trainable retarded children, each one can have one or two bells to play at the appropriate time. If you distribute the bells in this way, they make an excellent choice because the child does not have to decide or remember which bar or bars of all those on the instrument to play. Everyone can have the one task of playing his one or two notes in an ensemble on cues from you.

The child can also play a longer melodic fragment if you simplify it for him. For example, if the melody to be played is:

instead of having the bars of the resonator bells arranged according to ascending pitch (g, a, b, c, d), you can place them next to each other in the order they are to be played, from left to right—a, g, d, b, c.

Movement Activities

The severely retarded child enjoys movement activities. Start with the simplest movements. For example, nodding the head or tapping is simpler than clapping; clapping to music is simpler than walking or marching to music; and walking or marching is simpler than round or square dancing.

Older trainable retarded children can learn very simple square and round dances that require no special steps. These are excellent activities for coordination, following instructions, and paying attention to the caller. Playing the piano yourself or finding someone who can accompany these simple dances is better than using a recording because you can adjust the rate of speed to your group's abilities. It may be too difficult for them to remember or count the number of steps they are to take, and your emphasis should be on their responding to the music and your called instructions.

Song games and imitation games such as the ones described elsewhere in this chapter are useful not only for learning body parts and the meanings of verbs, but also for developing body control and working off tension. In these movement activities, moving to duple ($\frac{2}{4}$) meter is simpler for the trainable retarded than triple ($\frac{3}{4}$) meter, and tempos should not be too fast. Doing two things at the same time to music—walking and clapping, tapping desk and stamping feet—would be a difficult task for them.

A happy way to start the day is to have the children "parade" around the room to a Sousa march.

Listening Activities

Trainable retarded children can enjoy participating *actively* in music games, singing, and playing instruments for much longer times than one might expect (you will recall the band instrument lessons which lasted up to two-and-a-half hours), but because of their limited attention span, start with *very short listening periods* and very gradually increase them, perhaps up to two or three minutes. For perceptive listening, compositions should have very obvious structures and forms. The children should, at first, be asked to listen for one simple concept at a time, such as fast or slow, loud or soft, or whether they hear a man's or a woman's voice, etc. Speaking about their *personal* reactions should be encouraged.

Avoid having too much activity for the trainable retarded children during these brief listening times. Moving arms or hands in conducting movements or expressing the music with facial expression are enough. Otherwise, they may be so involved with moving around the floor that they will not be listening to the music. Retarded and emotionally disturbed children enjoy dissonance in music and respond to it, so music of this type should definitely be included. You may also want to experiment to see if any particular mood, tempo, beat, or dynamics level leads to less rocking and vocalizations or other uncontrolled autisms.

Miscellaneous Music Activities

A song like "This is the Way We Wash Our Hands" ("brush our teeth," "comb our hair," "sweep the floor," "say hello," etc.) is a fine one for practicing required habits and social skills. One teacher uses "The Anvil Chorus" from *Il Trovatore* as background music as the children practice brushing their teeth. Another states that the trainable mentally retarded with whom she worked did not respond to fire-drill signals with urgency until she played a recording of De Falla's "Ritual Fire Dance," an exciting composition with insistent, repetitive rhythms. She told them that it was "fire drill" music and they got on line quickly, impelled by the lively rhythm of the music. After many repetitions of this, they just had to hear the words "fire drill," and they would line up as quickly as they did when the music was being played.

You can use music throughout the day to make the child more aware of, and sensitive to, his environment. Does a school bell ring? Sing, "Ding-dong, hear the bell!" If someone enters briefly, you can sing, "Who was that? Who came in? Can you tell me, who was that?" The sounds of children laughing, an airplane overhead, a loud footstep—singing statements about them calls the children's attention to them, maximizes their sensory experiences, and gives names to events in their environment.

To make up for deficits in the short-term memory of the trainable retarded, special "rehearsal" techniques that have been used in teaching areas other than music can be of help. For example, because in learning to play a series of tones on several different resonator bells the child will tend to forget the first ones by the time he hears the last, have him practice the first two tones until they are well learned. As an example:

After the "G-E" sequence is learned, add the next "G," and practice that, always starting from the beginning. The next two tones (G-E) can be added, then the "A," always starting from the first two.

Sometimes, because of an apparent lack of ability, the trainable mentally retarded child is deprived of music. But for the sake of his self-image and because he can learn basic skills through the use of music, it is really an essential part of his education.

SUMMARY

Usually trainable mentally retarded children can perform and participate in the same music activities as normal children of the same mental age. In spite of the weakness in music memory and in performing or recognizing certain aspects of music, they have interest in and love for music. Studies show that their performance in other subject areas improves when music is used as a reward or as a teaching device, and a goodly number of them have learned by rote to play simple melodies on "real" instruments. In some cases, their attention span during individualized lessons has increased to more than two hours.

There are two basic purposes in using music with the trainable mentally retarded: helping the child achieve his music potential and using music to aid in teaching simple basic concepts and behaviors. By selecting and adapting music activities, for example, the teacher can help the trainable mentally retarded to play one-chord accompaniments on the autoharp and to participate in classroom music ensembles by playing one or two tones on resonator bells or very simple tunes on a melody flute.

Songs for these children should be meaningful to them and short in length and should, if possible, have universal appeal. It helps to pitch songs lower and to sing them slower than is usual for pupils with normal intelligence and to follow a set routine for music activities. Concepts such as direction (up and down, high and low, in and out, left and right), colors, body parts, and basic verbs as well as social skills can be taught or reinforced through the words of selected songs and music activities.

NOTES

[1]Kenneth Bruscia. "The Musical Characteristics of Mildly and Moderately Retarded Children," in *Readings: Developing Arts Programs for Handicapped Students.* (Arts in Special Education Project of Pennsylvania, 1981), p. 104.

[2]Betty Hunt Bradley, Marcel Hundziak and Ruth M. Patterson. *Teaching Moderately and Severely Retarded Children.* Springfield, Illinois: Charles C. Thomas, Publisher, 1971, p. 69.

[3]Phillip P. Strain and James E. Pierce. "Direct and Vicarious Effects of Social Praise on Mentally Retarded Preschool Children's Attentive Behavior," in *Readings in Trainable Mentally Handicapped.* Guilford, Connecticut: Special Learning Corp., 1980, pp. 57–61.

[4]Emily A. Stevens. "Some Effects of Tempo Changes on Stereotyped Rocking Movements of Low-Level Mentally Retarded Subjects." *American Journal of Mental Deficiency*, 76, No. 1 (1971), pp. 76–81.

[5]Diane McGunigle and Graham Bell. "Effects of Sedative and Stimulative Music on Activity Levels of Severely Retarded Boys." *American Journal of Mental Deficiency*, 75, No. 2 (1970), pp. 156–59.

[6]Sal Soraci, Jr., et al. "The Relationship Between Rate of Rhythmicity and Stereotypic Behaviors of Abnormal Children." *Journal of Music Therapy*, 19, No. 1 (Spring, 1982), p. 53.

[7]Marta Lienhard. "Factors Relevant to the Rhythmic Perception of a Group of Mentally Retarded Children." *Journal of Music Therapy*, 13, No. 2 (Summer, 1976), pp. 58–65.

[8]Martha L. Peters. "A Comparison of the Music Sensitivity of Mongoloid and Normal Children." *Journal of Music Therapy*, 7, No. 4 (Winter, 1970), pp. 113–23.

[9]Baldwin Electrosystems reports to music educators. Cincinnati, Ohio: Baldwin Music Education Division, 197[ ].

[10]Herbert D. Levin and Gail Levin. "Instrumental Music: A Great Aid in Promoting Self-Image," in *Music in Special Education.* Washington, D.C.: Music Educators National Conference, 1972, pp. 15–18.

[11]Robert F. Swift. "The Right Approach." *New York State School Music News*, 35, No. 7 (March, 1972), pp. 28–9.

[12]Paul Nordoff and Clive Robbins. *Music Therapy in Special Education.* New York: John Day Co., 1971, pp. 149ff.

[13]Karen Underhill. "The Effect of Contingent Music on Establishing Imitation in Behaviorally Disturbed Retarded Children." *Journal of Music Therapy*, 11, No. 3 (Fall, 1974), pp. 156–66.

[14]Martha Snead Holloway. "A Comparison of Passive and Active Music Reinforcement to Increase Preacademic and Motor Skills of Severely Retarded Children and Adolescents." *Journal of Music Therapy*, 17, No. 2 (Summer, 1980), pp. 58–69.

[15]Terrence Humphrey. "The Effect of Music Ear Training Upon Auditory Discrimination Abilities of Trainable Mentally Retarded Adolescents." *Journal of Music Therapy*, 17, No. 2 (Summer, 1980), pp. 70–74.

[16]E. Thayer Gaston, editor. *Music in Therapy*. New York: Macmillan Publishing Co., Inc., 1968, p. 60.

[17]Ibid., p. 60.

[18]Kenneth Bruscia. "The Musical Characteristics of Mildly and Moderately Mentally Retarded Children," p. 104.

[19]Mary Ellen Wylie. "Eliciting Vocal Responses in Severely and Profoundly Mentally Handicapped Subjects." *Journal of Music Therapy*, 20, No. 4 (Winter, 1983), pp. 190–200.

[20]Juliette Alvin. *Music for the Handicapped*, second edition. London: Oxford Press, 1976, p. 87.

CHAPTER ✗ 5

MUSIC FOR THE EDUCABLE MENTALLY RETARDED CHILD

An educable mentally retarded (EMR) child, with an I.Q. of from fifty-five to eighty, has impaired mental development that hinders educational performance. Because the EMR child functions primarily at the first and second stages of Piaget's theory—the sensorimotor and intuitive—he can be expected to make slower progress and to stay longer at each stage of development than the normal child.

Certain characteristics that the EMR child possesses which make learning difficult are of special significance for music instruction. Sensitive and somewhat emotionally insecure, and with feelings that are easily hurt, he needs encouragement, a feeling of achievement, and praise for any achievement. Thus, in music, as in other subjects, materials must be chosen that will give him the opportunity to learn and to succeed.

Though his attention span is short, interest can sometimes be awakened by adding music to classroom work. Because he reacts slowly to verbal instructions, he needs established routines and repetition to feel comfortable in classroom situations. This, plus the fact that language limitations result from a limited vocabulary, suggest that new words can be pleasantly introduced through songs and movement experiences because he welcomes frequent repetition—which can be the same sequence of the same songs. In addition, being less skillful verbally than the normal child, he is more interested in "doing" music than in talking about it.

Because he emotionally has the same *social* needs as children the same age of normal intelligence, his feelings are often offended by "baby stuff." At the same time, his intellectual ability limits the amount he can learn. This means that songs, listening activities, and instrument activities must be specially selected for him, but they must be those which are not obviously intended for younger children.

Frequently, he is very responsive to music, and while he may have less performance ability than the average child, he can accomplish more than one may surmise. A thirteen-year-old with an I.Q. of eighty to eighty-five has a mental age approximately equal to that of a ten-year-old or fifth grader. If the I.Q. of a thirteen-year-old is around fifty-five, the mental age is about seven years or that of the average second grader. Consider what a second-grade child can do: read, write, print, add, subtract, understand simple fractions and science concepts, learn songs, play simple melodies on musical instruments and learn basic music notation. And a fifth grader can learn to read and discuss news stories, write original compositions, understand division and multiplication, play more advanced compositions, etc. When we remember that a retarded child can perform at the level of his mental age, it is obvious that the educable mentally retarded cannot learn as much or as quickly as the normal child of the same age but he can make progress in learning music and can participate, at his own level, in a mainstreamed music class.

MUSICAL CHARACTERISTICS OF THE EDUCABLE MENTALLY RETARDED

Whatever abilities the educable mentally retarded may or may not have, one factor seems to be supported by teachers' experiences and a number of research studies: if musical aptitude is defined as musical expression, aural perception, love of music, and rhythmic response, then it is "relatively independent of intelligence or academic achievement and is but minimally related to various measures of . . . auditory abilities.[1] However, this is not the case when comparisons are made between the music *memory* of retarded children and that of children with normal intelligence. Given third-grade song material, for example, retarded youngsters with a chronological age of thirteen-and-a-half and a mental age equal to that of eight or nine years old remembers songs as well as the average third grader.[2] In a study in which melodic memory was tested, several hundred eight-year-old mentally retarded children with I.Q.'s of fifty to eighty-five were found to have approximately the same scores as several hundred five-year-olds.[3]

When it comes to learning a musical instrument, the educable retarded have shown an ability to achieve equal to that of other children of the same mental age. This was demonstrated in Sioux City, Iowa public schools in 1962, when a "special" brass band was formed. Starting with trumpet lessons and then branching out to instruction in learning trombones, sousaphones, drums, and bell-lyres, the children learned a whole series of pieces[4] and proudly performed them at P.T.A. meetings and for local organizations as well as at a convention of the National Association for Retarded Children.

Other instrumental programs for the educable mentally retarded have been equally successful with no significant difference noted between educable mentally handicapped and nonhandicapped children in learning to play wind instruments. So great is the motivation of these youngsters to learn an instrument that a short attention span, which is usually present in the retarded, does not appear to be a problem. In fact, many who have worked with them report that "the length of attention spans improved progressively as ... result of instrumental music participation."[5]

Given optimal teaching techniques, there is no reason not to have expectations of achievement in music for the educable mentally handicapped. This, however, does not mean that their accomplishments in music will equal that of children with normal and above-average intelligence with equal musical abilities. The musical capabilities of the retarded "appear unusually high only in comparison with their performance in more academic subjects: rarely are they as good as those of a normal child of the same age."[6] This is because the more one studies music, the more difficult it becomes. Complex theoretical concepts, rhythms requiring ability in handling fractions up to a sixty-fourth, understanding of performance practices and musical forms, more and more difficult musical notation, knowledge of the history of music—all of these, because of their high intellectual demands, limit the degree to which a mentally handicapped child can progress. But he can still derive much pleasure and self-satisfaction learning to play familiar melodies and participating with others in performing simple instrumentations.

As with the trainable mentally retarded, there is a difference between the singing voices of many educable mentally handicapped children and those of normal children. In a detailed study, Betsy Ann Larson found that the average range of singing voices of seven- and eight-year-old educable retarded children is significantly lower than that of normal children.[7] In addition, although there was overlapping in the voice ranges, the educable retarded child is more comfortable singing within a smaller range. For example:

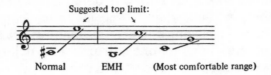

Normal   EMH   (Most comfortable range)

Fortunately, with slight adaptations and some special activities, most educable mentally handicapped children can participate in all aspects of the regular elementary school music curriculum—singing, listening, movement, playing instruments, and creating music. "What the child can't *understand*, he can still *do* and enjoy."[8]

MUSIC IN RELATIONSHIP TO THE CLASSROOM CURRICULUM

Experiments and studies have repeatedly shown that when music lessons are incorporated into the training of slow learners, their learning improves. Not only do they learn more easily, but they also are able to remember more if it is taught rhythmically and tunefully. What is more, peripheral benefits can be derived, including classroom control, increased attention, and more self-reliance.

Sometimes, these benefits appeared to result directly from the musical experiences themselves. For example, when material suitable for the third grade was presented to thirteen-year-old retarded children as story, as poetry, or in song, the songs were remembered better than the stories and the stories better than the poems.[9]

Among the most serious problems teachers have to face is helping the child who reads below grade level. A number of recent studies have attempted to determine what effects, if any, music instruction or the actual incorporation of music into the Language Arts curriculum would have on reading scores, reading readiness, language development, and sound-symbol recognition.

In Linda Kelly's study, first-grade children were assigned to groups which met three times a week for six months.[10] One group, made up of children at the lower reading level, was given instruction in what is called "Orff Schulwerk." Developed by the composer Carl Orff, this is a program which includes rhythmic response, word chants, and creative instrumental activities. By the end of the program, these children had improved enough in reading and related areas so that they reached the level of the other children.

One of the most dramatic experiments was done by Diana Nicholson. She used 50 children, aged six to eight, who were slow learners with I.Q.'s of eighty to ninety-five, and taught them through a special program that included body movement to illustrate concepts of slow and fast and high and low, singing alphabetical tones, controlling mood through music, and listening to records—at first for one minute and then gradually increasing the time span to five minutes.[11] The control group, also consisting of slow learners, had an "average" music program which was not as creative. It did not include learning to read music, using music to control mood, or the same work in increasing the listening attention time span.

At the end of the school year, the improvement in the experimental group was marked. Their average pretest score in reading was 1.22; the post-test average was 3.77. The control group started at the same level and by the end of the year, their average score was only 1.38.

In 1967, Esther Seides tried to discover whether adolescents, talented in music but slow in learning to read, would improve in reading and mathematical achievement if given music lessons.[12] She selected 84 students at an inner-city junior high school in New York. Most of them were educably mentally handicapped and all had I.Q.'s of seventy-five to ninety and read at least two years below grade level. They were divided into three groups. Some musically talented pupils were placed in a "regular" (i.e., no music) class. Some talented pupils were placed in a music talent class. And there was a group of non-talented pupils placed in a "regular" class. One year later, when they were retested, the slow learners talented in music who were given music lessons showed the greatest achievement in arithmetic, reading, and creativity. Their self-image was higher and their average Work Knowledge and Reading scores were 5.7 and 5.6 respectively, compared to the other groups' 4.7 and 4.8.

Other researchers have determined that when music instruction is given as a reward for achievement in class work, it can be effective. Then, the children's desire to learn the music provided the motivation for them to try harder to accomplish more in their regular school work.

In Michael Gordon's experiment, he selected 54 fourth graders from each of two inner-city school districts. Half of these pupils in each school—those reading on grade level—were not given music lessons. The other half, the experimental group of children who were given lessons on band instruments, were slow learners and at least one year delayed in reading.

At first, the experimental group was given music lessons regularly. In the next phase, in order to receive a music lesson, a child in the experimental group had to meet individual criteria in reading and classroom behavior. In other words, instruction in music was a reward. While there were significant differences between the two groups in reading ability at the pre-test, there was none at the post-test. Music instruction provided excellent motivation for increasing actual daily reading performance.[13]

The same sort of result occurred when televised music lessons were used with educable mentally handicapped children as a reward for correct mathematical responses.[14] Their mathematics test scores improved. Also, when music selected by the children in the fifth grade who were involved in the study was used as a reward for "paying attention" to mathematics lessons,[15] while there was no marked improvement in the high and middle ability groups of thirty children each, *the lowest ability group had a significant increase in correct mathematics responses.*

This motivating force of music as a reward and as a teaching technique has long been noted by parents and teachers. There are the mother who writes that her fourteen-year-old son was not doing well in school and hated to read until she had him sing the words printed on the sleeves of popular record albums,[16] and the mother who was finally able to teach their address to her little kindergarten boy by singing it to him.[17]

A college student-teacher states that the small group of retarded children she was tutoring became bored and restless while she was trying to teach them the sight word "apple." "Suddenly it came to me," she writes. "I thought I would try making up a song about an apple. [The children's] response was wonderful and I had their complete attention. I made up a short lyric:

> An apple is green.
> An apple is red.
> And Kwame, Mascine and Gary should have one
> Before they go to bed.

"I have no idea what melody I used but the children loved it. As a matter of fact, they were [still] singing [it] at lunch time."[18]

Why do music lessons help slow learners? Because of music's great appeal, it may be able to hold the child's attention. Anything that combats interference or distraction or forces attention to the task at hand increases the ability to remember. Or perhaps it is the multi-sensory approach possible in teaching music through movement and eye–ear–body coordination that is the factor that helps. In addition, certain basic principles and practices in music and language reading involve the same connections between eye and ear understanding: the words of a song are read from left to right and from one line to the next. In order to sing the words correctly, it is necessary to know how to divide them into syllables and to know which syllables to emphasize. Thus, additional highly motivating practice in reading can be provided.

Many teachers are concerned about the effects mainstreaming educable mentally retarded children will have on the learning of the normal children in the class, fearing that the handicapped children will slow down the others. Music classes, because they allow for variety in the levels of activities, are frequently "mainstreamed." Barbara Force conducted a study in which she compared two first-grade music classes. One had no retarded children; the other had several. After the classes had about a month of music lessons, it was found that there was no difference in learning in the two classes. The normal children were not at all affected by having retarded children in class with them. "Regardless of classification, both groups increased significantly from pre- to post-test" in their knowledge of music, she writes. ". . . all children showed learning."[19]

Apparently, music activities can be adapted to enable children with varying intellectual abilities to participate and learn together. The classroom and music teacher can work with the confidence and faith that music can contribute to aesthetically improving the lives of all children.

MUSIC ACTIVITIES

In teaching music to EMR children, the same basic principles should be used as with TMR children: a noncompetitive environment, encouragement and approval for progress in learning, repetition and routine, concrete examples, and a multi-sense approach.

Singing Activities

1. If possible, use songs that have natural speech emphasis. By having the emphasis in the music and the word accents fall on the same tone, reading can be improved. After the child learns the words

of a song by rote and then reads them, he will understand better how the words are divided into syllables and where to put the word accents.

2. Pick songs that are not too fast. The slower learner needs time to enunciate words. As the song becomes more familiar, the tempo (rate of speed) can be increased, where appropriate.

3. Avoid songs that are either *too* serious or *too* exciting. The first can cause lack of interest; the second, too much stimulation. It is a good idea to have a variety of songs and moods—funny, gentle, lively, rousing, sedative.

4. Select songs that the EMR child can enjoy singing together with others. Third- and fourth-grade song books usually have a lot of songs that appeal to many ages and intelligence levels (for example, "Michael, Row the Boat Ashore," "Marching to Praetoria," "Kum-Ba-Yah," "Home on the Range") and these are also suitable for educable retarded children.

5. The interests of the child should be considered in selecting songs. Simple melodies and texts, such as those found in folk songs, can encourage the greatest participation. But a song about "See the Little Bunny Go Hop, Hop" would be an insult to an educable mentally handicapped eight-year-old with a mental age of a five-year-old.

6. Where there is a song with many verses and complexities, it is better if the song has a refrain. In this way, until a child is able to remember all the words, he can always sing the chorus.

7. It may be necessary to change the words in a song to make it comprehensible. However, many songs can provide the opportunity for increasing the children's vocabulary. Your judgment must be your guide.

8. Songs can be sung "a cappella" (with no accompaniment) or together with records or with an autoharp, piano, or guitar accompaniment. If you play the piano, try to sit so that the children can see your face and enunciate the words carefully. Both of these will help the educable retarded child to learn the words more easily.

9. Keep in mind that the register of the educable mentally retarded child's voice is lower than the average, therefore pitch the songs accordingly. Because there is overlapping in the vocal ranges of the educable retarded and those of normal intelligence, all should be comfortable singing within the following range:

SONGS FOR A LIMITED VOCAL RANGE

"Ostinato" songs are enjoyable for all and can be very helpful if you are singing part-songs or if there are children in the class who have very limited ranges or low-pitched voices. An ostinato is a small fragment of melody repeated over and over (it is "obstinate") while the main melody is sung at the same time. Examples are:

SARASPONDA
(Spinning Song)

(The ostinato represents the humming of the spinning wheel.)

ZUM GALI GALI

Israeli Folk Song

(Sing the ostinato twice as an introduction to the song, then sing throughout.)

English translation

1. The worker is a pioneer, the pioneer is a worker.
2. Peace is for all nations; all [Mankind] is for peace.

Ostinatos can be added to some of the "one-chord" songs found in Chapter 4. For example:

Ostinato for "Swing Low, Sweet Chariot"　　　　Last measure

Cha-ri-ot is com-in', Cha-ri-ot is com-in'. Come!

Ostinato for "There's A Little Wheel A-Turning"

'Round and 'round, go 'round and 'round, 'Round and 'round, go 'round and 'round.

In addition to ostinato songs, include some songs among those you teach to the whole class that children with a limited vocal range can sing. Start at the pitch level shown to be most comfortable for the educable mentally retarded (　　　　) and gradually make it higher over a period of time. Some songs with limited range are:

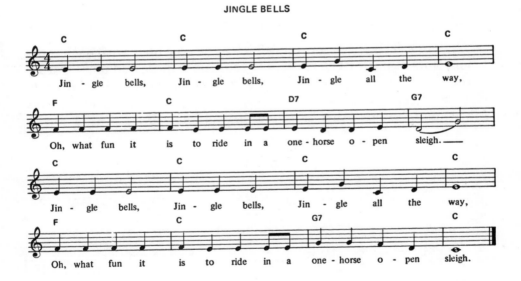

JINGLE BELLS

Jin-gle bells, Jin-gle bells, Jin-gle all the way,

Oh, what fun it is to ride in a one-horse o-pen sleigh. ——

Jin-gle bells, Jin-gle bells, Jin-gle all the way,

Oh, what fun it is to ride in a one-horse o-pen sleigh.

Note: This version of "Jingle Bells" is pitched lower than the usual arrangement for the average child's voice, but well within the range of most voices.

GO TELL AUNT RHODIE

2. The one she was saving,
   The one she was saving,
   The one she was saving,
   To make a feather bed.

3. It died in the mill pond. . . .
   From standing on its head.

For some additional songs with limited range, see the Correlative Song Chart, beginning on page xi.

SONGS TO CHALLENGE AND IMPROVE THE MEMORY

A "cumulative" song is one which adds new lines with each repetition, thus requiring the singers to remember more and more words. If the words are added in different sequence each time, the challenge is greater. Probably, among the best known of this type is "Old McDonald." Some other examples are as follows:

THE TREE IN THE WOODS

English Folk Song

Verse 2:   All in a woods there stands a tree,
The finest tree you ever did see,
And a limb was on the tree, and
the tree was in the woods,
And the green grass grew. . . .

Verse 3:   And a branch was on the limb,
and the limb was on the tree, and
the tree was in the woods . . .

Verse 4:   And a nest was on the branch, and
the branch was on the limb . . .

Verse 5:   And an egg was in the nest, and
the nest was on the branch . . .

Verse 6:   And a bird was on the egg . . .

Verse 7:   And a wing was on the bird . . .

Verse 8:   And a feather was on the wing . . .

Verse 9:   And a spot was on the feather . . .

OLD KING COLE

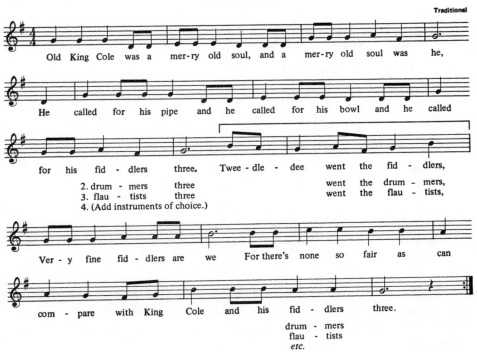

Each time the song is sung, sing the parts for the previous instruments. Names of rhythm band instruments can be used, with the children playing at the appropriate times.

SHE'LL BE COMIN' 'ROUND THE MOUNTAIN

Verse 2: She'll be drivin' six white horses when she comes.

Verse 3: Oh, we'll all go out to meet her when she comes.

Verse 4: Then we'll kill the old red rooster when she comes.

Verse 5: And we'll all have chicken and dumplings when she comes.

Spoken Words	Motions
Verse 1:	Pull imaginary train whistle for each "toot."
Verse 2:	Pull on reins.
Verse 3:	Wave hand.
Verse 4:	Flap arms like wings.
Verse 5:	Rub stomach.

At the end of each verse, add the sounds and gestures of previous verses. The last words will be, "We'll all have chicken and dumplings when she comes, Yum, Yum! Cock-a-doodle-doo! Hi, there! Whoa back! Toot toot!"

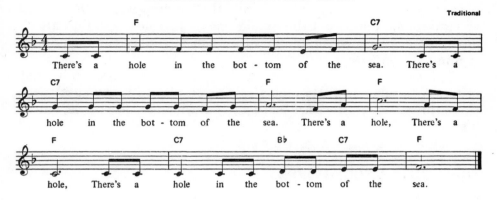

THERE'S A HOLE IN THE BOTTOM OF THE SEA

Verse 2: There's a log on the hole in the
bottom of the sea . . .

Verse 3: There's a bump on the log on the
hole in the bottom of the sea . . .

Verse 4: There's a frog on the bump on the
log on the hole in the bottom . . .

Verse 5: There's a leg on the frog on the
bump on the log on the hole . . .

Verse 6: There's a spot on the leg on the
frog on the bump on the log on
the hole . . .

Verse 7: There's a speck on the spot on the
leg on the frog on the bump . . .

Classroom Instruments Activities

The tonette and melody flute would be the optimum classroom wind
instruments for the educable mentally retarded. While their tone
quality is not as satisfying as that of the recorder, the same melodies
can be played. In addition, the youngsters who cannot cope with recorders can have the opportunity to learn some familiar as well as
unfamiliar melodies and to expand their knowledge of music. In this
way, they can feel pride in their accomplishments.

Those children who can't read music can learn to play by rote—
imitating you and the other children (shadowing) and by actually
having help in placing fingers in the correct position (positioning).

You can prepare charts or work sheets on which the names of the notes to be played are printed. While the children who have learned to read music play from the music scores, the slower children who have not yet learned simple notation can also play the melody by reading the letters.

The simplest tones to learn are "g, a, and b"—taught in that order. A number of little melodies can be played using just these three tones. When these are learned, you can add other tones, one at a time.

Some three-note songs are as follows:

RIDE A COCK-HORSE

Ride a cock-horse——
G   AB   A

To Ban-bu-ry Cross,——
A G   A B   A

To see a fine la-dy
A G   AB AG

Ride on a white horse.——
G   AB A   G

HOT CROSS BUNS

Hot cross buns,
B   A   G

Hot cross buns,
B   A   G

One, a pen-ny, two a pen-ny,
G   GG   G, A   AA   A

Hot cross buns.
B   A   G

MARY HAD A LITTLE LAMB

Ma-ry had a lit-tle lamb,
B AG ABB B

Lit-tle lamb, lit-tle lamb.
A A A   B B B

Ma-ry had a lit-tle lamb,
B AG AB B B,

Its fleece was white as snow.
B   A   A   B   AG

AU CLAIR DE LA LUNE

Au clair de la lu-ne,
G G   G A B A

Mon a-mi Pier-rot.
G   BA A G

Pre-tez moi ta plu-me,
G G G   A B A

Pour é-crire un mot.
G   BA   A G

TROLLEY SONG

Ding, ding, ding, went the trol-ley.——
B   B   B   A G A B

Ding, ding, ding, went the bell———
B   B   B   A G A

Ding, ding, ding, went my heart-strings——
B   B   B   A G A B

For the mo-ment I saw him I fell.
G   A B G   AB G A G

LET THE SUN SHINE IN

Let the sun shine in,
B—B B A   A——

Let the sun shine in,
A——A A G   G——

Let the sun shine in,
B—B B A   A——
The——sun shine in.
G A B A   G

"Hokey-pokey" is a popular four-note song and there are so many five-tone melodies (e.g., "Jingle Bells," "Duke of York," "Lightly Row," "Ode to Joy" theme from Beethoven's *Ninth Symphony*, "Go Tell Aunt Rhodie," "Going Home" theme from Dvorak's *New World Symphony*) that a large repertoire can be built using only the tones "g, a, b, c, and d."

Playing Other Melody Instruments

Because each bar of the melody bells (also called "song bells") has the name of its tone indicated on it and it is played by striking the bars with a mallet, it does not require very fine motor coordination or remembering where to place the fingers. It is therefore easier to play than any of the classroom wind instruments. Here again, you can start with simple three-note melodies. Some children who have difficulty playing any of the classroom wind instruments may be more successful with melody bells. The resonator bells can also be used very successfully with educable retarded children.

Some simple, delightful activities are based on the "Orff Schulwerk" method. One of the most important contributions Carl Orff, the twentieth century German composer and music educator, made was the development of his creative approach to teaching music. The pentatonic scale is used in this method not only to develop creativity but in learning specially composed and arranged music based on the pentatonic scale.

By playing a rhythmic pattern on the black bars of the song bells or resonator bells in any order at all, a melody will result. You are using the tones of the pentatonic (five-tone) scale. Notice that on any keyboard, the pattern of two black and three black note groups keeps repeating. Each group of black keys makes up a pentatonic scale, as shown in Figure 5-1.

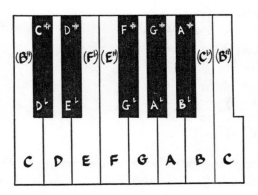

Figure 5-1

For some reason, the music of many people, including American-Indian, Japanese, Chinese, Scottish, Afro-American, Hungarian, and African, as well as many American folk and popular tunes, are frequently based on tunes which can be played on the black keys of a piano.

Give the children many opportunities to improvise pentatonic melodies. This is a fine activity for retarded children because the results are so immediately satisfying, thus enhancing self-image. In addition, little instruction and absolutely no ability to read music is required at the start for the simplest "Orff" activities. At the same time, hand–eye coordination, creativity, and relationships with others through ensemble playing can be developed.

Some simple activities using the pentatonic scale are as follows:

PLAY QUESTIONS AND ANSWERS ON THE SONG BELLS

Use two sets of song bells or resonator bells. Mark the F sharp (F# is the first black note immediately above F) with white chalk. Distribute the bells to two children. The first child creates a pentatonic melody using the black bars and ending on any bar except the F#. The second child plays an "answer" based on the pentatonic scale, ending on F#. It is helpful to establish a rhythmic pattern for the melody before starting to improvise, but this is not necessary.

PLAY PENTATONIC DUETS

Use two sets of melody bells, or melody and resonator bells. Have one child play an ostinato by repeating a small rhythmic fragment of melody again and again. As the ostinato is played on one set of bells, a second child improvises a pentatonic melody on the other set of bells.

PLAY ACCOMPANIMENTS FOR PENTATONIC MELODIES

Play simple arrangements of pentatonic melodies by accompanying them using simple ostinatos. The children can make up their own ostinatos using three or more tones of the pentatonic scale in playing the melody or resonator bells.

The black keys are not the only combination of tones that can form a pentatonic chord. There are many other pentatonic scales. Among the simplest are the following:

C, D, E, G, A

F, G, A, C, D

G, A, B, D, E

You will find that if these five-tone groups are combined in almost any way, a pleasant melody will result.

Some "sample" pentatonic melodies are:

GOODBYE OLD PAINT

Cowboy Song

Good - bye, Old Paint, I'm a - leav - in' Chey - enne.

1. { My   foot   in   the   stir - rup, my   po - ny won't stand, __
     I'm a - leav - in' Chey - enne, _____ I'm   off   for Mon - tan'. __

2. { I'm a - rid - in' Old Paint, _____ I'm a - lead - in' old Dan, __
     Good - bye, to the   old ranch, I'm a- leav - in' Chey - enne. _____

CINDY

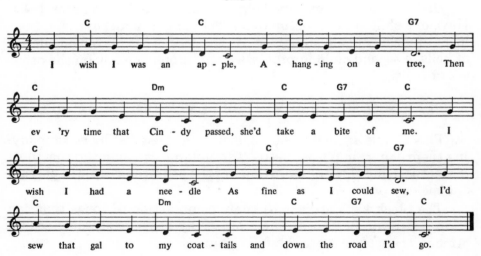

I   wish   I   was   an   ap - ple, A - hang - ing   on   a   tree, Then

ev - 'ry   time   that   Cin - dy   passed, she'd   take   a   bite   of   me.   I

wish   I   had   a   nee - dle   As   fine   as   I   could   sew,   I'd

sew   that   gal   to   my   coat - tails   and   down   the   road   I'd   go.

The arrangements given above for "Goodbye, Old Paint" and "Cindy" are both based on the C pentatonic scale. Therefore, when adding ostinatos to these melodies, distribute the resonator bells bars marked C, D, E, G, and A. Many well-known songs are based on pentatonic scales, and a number of these can be found in this book. (See the Correlative Song Chart for examples.) In addition, a goodly number can be harmonized with one chord (for example, "Swing Low, Sweet Chariot," "A Hole in the Bucket"). Thus, some children can be singing while others play rhythm instruments or the autoharp. A few could be playing simple ostinatos.

If a child can't remember his part, just as for the trainable retarded child, you can, if necessary, rearrange the bars of a short melodic phrase so that they will be placed, left to right, in the order they are to be played rather than according to ascending pitch. This makes it easier for the child to play the correct bars.

Accompanying with the autoharp: Some children have trouble locating the specific bars for chords when more than one or two chords are used to harmonize a melody. In those cases, playing the auto-harp can be made very simple through the use of color coding. If, for example, the three chords G, C, D^7 are needed, circle all the G chord indications with red crayon, the C's with yellow, and the D^7's with a different color. Then, using washable markers, color the light portion of the G, C, and D^7 bars with the matching colors. In this way, the child sees the color in the music score and pushes the button of the same color on the autoharp.

Playing the Swiss melody bells: Draw blocks of color to represent the colored Swiss melody bells; each note will be represented by its own color (see Figure 5-2). This can be done using a chart or by pre-paring special scores for the children who need them. The children stand in a row, each one holding a different bell. Then reading left to right, they play the bells in turn, as indicated by the colored blocks.

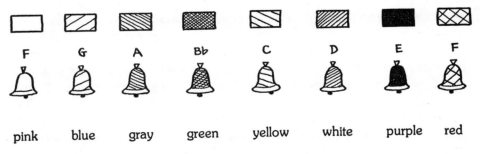

Figure 5-2

This activity also emphasizes that reading proceeds from left to right and helps to review matching and recognition of colors.

Playing rhythm instruments: Educable retarded children can participate in almost all rhythm band activities together with other children. These can range from creative improvisations (see the activities in Chapter 2 dealing with music for emotionally disturbed children for some suggestions), to deciding which instruments best fit a song or orchestra composition, to playing a set pattern. Deciding which rhythm instrument is suitable and how to play it should take into consideration a number of factors such as how loud or soft the music is, whether a "banging" or "shaking" instrument would be best, whether the melody is the same all the way through the music or if there are different sections which should be treated differently, and whether the ethnic origins of the music should help to determine the instruments selected. Maracas, castanets, bongos, and guiros could be used for Latin-American songs; tone blocks and finger cymbals for Oriental, etc. Drums and cymbals would be appropriate for a march; finger cymbals and triangles for quiet music.

Some children can play the rhythm of the melody, some a "counter" (that is, different) rhythm. Children who cannot remember a rhythmic pattern can play on all the beats or just on the strong beat.

As in all rhythm band activities *for all children*, avoid distributing too many instruments (seven or eight may be enough). Otherwise, the music being accompanied will be "drowned out" and chaos can result. The children can learn to take turns; they will remember who played the drums last! For older children, use instruments most like real ones.

Playing in a classroom ensemble: As stated, both trainable and educable retarded children can participate in playing classroom instruments, and appropriate arrangements have been made using song bells, resonator bells, the autoharp, a recorder, the voice, and rhythm instruments. In the two arrangements that follow, notice the simplicity of some of the parts as compared to the more complicated wind instrument part. Certainly, a trainable retarded child could easily play the one bar required for the resonator bells in "The Farmer in the Dell." The children who have learned to read music and to play the recorder or melody flute could play the melody. In "Cindy," color coding could be used, if desired, to simplify the autoharp chords and rhythm instruments could play accompanying rhythms of varying degrees of difficulty:

THE FARMER IN THE DELL

CINDY

Listening Activities

Several basic approaches are useful in conducting listening lessons with educable retarded children, as follows:

1. If the children are not engaging in concurrent activities (such as moving or drawing to music) and are just listening, start with very short works—perhaps a minute or two in length—and gradually increase the listening time.

2. When asking the children to listen perceptively for specific aspects of the music, always let them know ahead of time what to listen for. Otherwise, their responses may change the lesson into a guessing game. It is also a good idea to limit the number of things to notice in the music to a few facets and to the more obvious ones. As they become more used to this type of activity and develop more perceptivity, it may be possible to have them listen for more items.

3. Keep discussion time brief. If the concept being taught is, for example, ABA form (a first melody or section of music followed by a contrasting one and then a return to the original music), let the children have *experiences* to help them feel and perceive the changes and repetitions in the music—such as drawing patterns to illustrate the different qualities of the A and B sections, creating dances for A and B to express the form, or conducting in their seats. Average and bright children may be interested in talking about the differences between the A and B sections, but for the educable retarded, this can lead to restlessness.

4. Vary the activities. Perhaps when listening to the instruments of the orchestra, at one lesson they could pantomime playing the instrument heard; another time, they could select and circle the pictures of the instruments.

5. Most children, including the educable retarded, are fascinated by real instruments and love "live" performances. Whenever possible, include these. It is usually possible to invite friends or family members of the children in your class or from other classes to play for the children.

Teaching Music Reading and Concepts

The educable retarded can participate fully in many music activities —developing the sense of pitch and the sense of rhythm, body movement, singing, rhythm band activities, vocal chants; none of these present serious problems. They can also learn to play simple music on classroom as well as band instruments and piano or guitar. However, actually reading notes, remembering rhythm notation and learning theoretical concepts can be more difficult. Just as the slow learner will take longer to learn to read language, you can expect that the educable retarded child will take longer to learn to read music notation.

In a homogeneous class of educable mentally retarded children, there would not be as many problems as there would be in a mainstreamed class. This is because the retarded would all be learning at approximately the same rate. A very bright child, however, can understand and remember basic music notation—meaning of the staff, names of notes on lines and spaces, simple rhythm notation and counting—in just a few lessons, while an average child will take a little longer, and an educable mentally handicapped child may need several lessons just to be able to tell whether a note is on a line or inside a space.

If you are working only with the educable mentally retarded, many approaches are needed. Fortunately, for this you can call upon a large number of music reading activities and attractive games designed for all children. These include body movement, board games, floor staffs, word chants, wall staffs, simple paper and pencil activities, puzzles, team games, flash cards, music notation "Bingo" and spin-the-arrow games, and jigsaw puzzles. This variety can prevent the numerous repetitions required to teach the subject matter from becoming boring and also provide the needed multi-sense appeal.

In a class consisting of average, bright, and educable retarded children, there is the question of what to do when most of the children can read music and the retarded have not yet learned to do so, and also when the educable mentally handicapped children's language reading performance is that of younger children. If one or two varied review activities are incorporated into the music lessons, the slow learners can have additional help in learning music notation while the interest of the other children is still maintained. In the meantime, by using some of the activities previously suggested in this chapter, the educable retarded can participate by performing on wind instruments, song and resonator bells, the autoharp and rhythm instruments, without yet knowing how to read music.

In music lessons for which the aim is to apprehend music concepts, it is possible for the slow learner to have experiences without intellectualization. When the class is learning about music or engaging in music activities that require reading or writing skills, the educable retarded children can still be involved in the lesson on their own level without being singled out.

For example, if the concepts being taught are dynamics in music and the symbols "p," "pp," "f," "ff," etc., the activity can be to make lists of sounds and to write next to each one the dynamics symbol that would best describe each sound. At the same time, the child who has difficulty writing out lists can draw pictures or bring them in and paste them onto a chart with appropriately labelled columns.

The same thing can be done in teaching about tempo indications: some children can make lists of moving objects and next to each one write the name of the tempo of its movement. Others can make a chart labelled with various tempo indications and draw or paste pictures of things which move at these different rates of speed.

Similar modifications of activities can be developed for lessons about high and low sounds and for other music symbols and concepts for which pictures or body movement can be stressed.

MUSIC ACTIVITIES AS AN AID IN TEACHING THE CLASSROOM CURRICULUM

"Because it adds pleasure to learning and enhances motivation and interest, music can enhance learning in many areas of the curriculum and at all grade levels. It can become a highly valuable, integral part of the teaching and learning process."[20] This is especially true for retarded children who, you will recall, best remember subject matter when it is presented in song. Rhythmic chants and songs used throughout the school day can help to reinforce subject matter. Take, for example, the song "This Old Man":

THIS OLD MAN

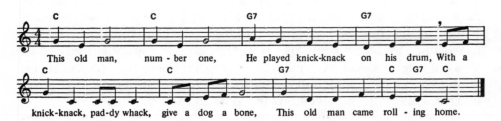

Number two, he played knick-knack on a shoe.
. . . three, he played knick-knack on a tree.
. . . four, ... on the door, etc.

If, in mathematics, the children are dealing with sets and number recognition, you can prepare attractive charts, each one showing a different number of objects. On one, there might be six stars; on another, three drums; on a third, eight dolls or circles. As the children sing, they would not know which number will come next until after the opening words "This old man. . . ." are sung. Then one of the charts would be displayed and the children would demonstrate their recognition of the number of objects they see by singing the appropriate words.

During daily reading lessons, each child can receive a copy of the words of "This Old Man" (or another favorite, well-known song) printed on stiff oak-tag and cut into pieces to form a jigsaw puzzle. Then, as they put the parts together, they would not only be dealing with the relationship of the shapes and reading the familiar words, but they would also be recalling the song's cheerful melody. They would be "feeling it in their hearts," as one child said. Or the children can draw pictures showing their conception of how "This Old Man" could possibly play "knick-knack." Thus, music can become an integral part of their school work.

A number of songs can aid in teaching mathematical concepts such as rote counting, subtraction, or multiplication. For example:

(For Sets and Rote Counting)

THE ELEPHANT SONG

One el-e-phant be-gan to play, Up-on a spi-der's web one day,
He thought it such a lot of fun, He asked an-oth-er el-e-phant to come.

Additional verses:

> Two elephants began to play. . . .
> Three elephants began to play. . . .
> Four elephants began to play, etc.

(Multiplying by Two's)

FOUR IN A BOAT

1. One
2. Two   } in a boat and the tide rolls high,   { One / Two / Four } in a boat and the tide rolls high,
3. Four

{ One / Two / Four } in a boat and the tide rolls high, Get you a pret-ty one bye and bye.

Words	Motions
1. One in a boat and the tide rolls high, (3 times) Get you a pretty one bye and bye.	Children walk in circle, one child in center.
2. Choose a partner stay all day, (3 times)	Children stand in circle; child in center picks and stands in front of a partner.
We don't care what the old folks say.	Child who was in center brings partner to center of circle.
3. Two in the boat and it won't go 'round, (3 times) Swing with the pretty one you just found.	Children in center swing as others clap hands.

(Repeat with two, then four, then eight in center.)

(Ordinal Numbers)

THE THREE CROWS

Scottish Song

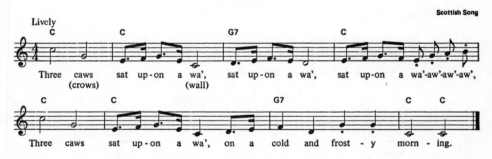

2. The first caw could na' (not) find his maw (mother). . . . (3 times)
   On a cold and frosty morning.

3. The second caw could na' find his paw (father). . . . (3 times)
   On a cold and frosty morning.

4. The third caw ate the other twa (two). . . . (3 times)
   On a cold and frosty morning.

COUNTING SONG
(To the tune of Twinkle, Twinkle, Little Star)

One, two, trhee, four, five, six, seven, I can see the stars in heav'n.
Eight, nine, ten, e - lev - en, twelve, I can say them by my - self.
One, two, three, four, five, six, sev'n, I can see the stars in heav'n.

Other counting verses to "Twinkle, Twinkle, Little Star" can be:

Counting by Two's

Two, four, six, eight, and ten,
Can you sing these words again?
Twelve, fourteen, sixteen, eighteen,
Next comes twenty—that is plenty.
Two, four, six, eight and ten,
Can you sing these words again?

Counting by Three's

Three, and, six, and nine, and twelve,
I can say them by myself.
Fifteen, eighteen, and there's more,
Twenty-one, then twenty-four.
Three, and six, and nine, and twelve,
I have said them by myself.

(Rote Counting)

THE ANGEL BAND

Southern Folk Song

There was one, there were two, there were three lit - tle an - gels, There were four, there were four, there were six, lit - tle an-gels, There were sev - en, there were eight, there were nine lit - tle an - gels, Ten lit - tle an-gels in the band. _____ Was-n't that a band, Sun - day morn - ing, Sun - day morn - ing, Sun - day morn - ing, Was-n't that a band Sun - day morn - ing, Sun - day morn - ing soon? _____

(Repeat first section)

The song, "Ten in the Bed" provides good practice in counting backwards. When "none in the bed" is reached, you can have the children sing, "Roll back, roll back. So they all rolled back and one came in, there was one in the bed. . . ." and so on, and on, and on. . . .

TEN IN THE BED

For excellent reading practice, project a transparency showing the words of a favorite song. Then, as the class sings the song, either you or one of the children can use a pencil to point to the words on the transparency. You will usually find that the youngster will try to read and follow the words with intense concentration.

Some reading readiness activities are given in Chapter 3 on music for the learning disabled. Some others can be singing the song "My Bonnie Lies Over the Ocean," and raising hands every time a word beginning with the letter "B" is sung; forming letters of the alphabet, such as "O," "Y," "I," "C," "J," "G," etc., with arms and singing to the tune of "Hokey-Pokey" ("I make myself an A/ I make myself an A/ I give myself a shake, shake, shake/ And turn myself around"). For the older child who already knows how to read and write, titles such as "Where Did Music Come From?" "If I Were a Violin," or "My Favorite Singer" can motivate efforts at creative writing.

A game of "musical concentration" can serve both to enhance memory and provide reading practice. For this, write the names of song titles on cards and cut the cards in half. With the cards placed face downwards, one of the children selects two of them at random, trying to piece together the title of a song. If he has guessed correctly, the children sing the song and the game continues. If he has not found the two halves of a title, the cards are replaced in the original position and another child has a turn. The object of the game is to remember the position of each card and to pick the two that can form a title. Intense concentration is needed for this game. You can start with just two titles and gradually increase to three or four as the youngsters become more skillful.

A variation of "musical chairs" can add fun to lessons in many areas of the curriculum. The children stand in a circle as music is played and pass a card on which is written an arithmetic problem, a word that they are learning, a sentence to read, or a question about science or social science, etc. When the music is stopped, the child holding the card answers the question or reads the words.

The more times you use music as an alternative means in teaching the school curriculum, the easier it will be for you to think of other activities. There are resources that stress an activities approach in teaching music notation and music concepts and that offer suggestions for using music to teach the classroom curriculum. These are listed in the Appendix.

Whether you are using music to teach aspects of the school curriculum or to add pleasure and beauty to the school day, or teaching the children how to sing songs, play musical instruments, or understand music concepts, it is important to offer encouragement and praise to the educable retarded for any progress they make and to give them step-by-step tasks that they are capable of learning.

SUMMARY

Although educable retarded children make slower progress and stay longer at each stage of development than normal children, they can be expected eventually to achieve most of the skills taught in the elementary school music curriculum.

Sensitive and with feelings easily hurt, they need to have a sense of achievement and belonging. Although they may not understand intellectually many aspects of music and their music memory is poorer than that of the average child, they are frequently more successful in music activities than in other subject areas. Many studies have shown a direct relationship between learning to read music and improvement in language reading.

Songs selected for these children should have natural speech emphasis and include many selections that can be enjoyed by all grades and by children of the same chronological age. Songs with refrains, pitched a little lower than usual, and with the melody within a limited range are most successful. Part-singing of simple rounds and "ostinatos" can be enjoyed by older educable mentally retarded children, and many songs can help to reinforce concepts in language arts and mathematics.

The educable mentally retarded child can be expected to learn to read simple music, although it may take much longer than it does for the average child. Many varied activities to teach music reading should be used so that the child will not feel that he is "dumb." Step-by-step procedures, starting with two- and three-note melodies played by rote and then gradually introducing music reading and more and more notes, can be used in teaching melody instruments such as tonette and melody flute. Resonator bars can be rearranged to make a tune easier to play. Autoharp accompaniments can be "color coded" to enable the child to perform without difficulty.

With slight modifications, the educable retarded child can enjoy most music activities even if he cannot understand the theoretical aspects.

NOTES

[1]John Bixler. "Musical Aptitude in the Educable Mentally Retarded Child." *Journal of Music Therapy*, 5, No. 2 (June, 1968), p. 43.

[2]Wanda Bea Lathom. "Retarded Children's Retention of Songs, Stories, and Poems." (Unpublished doctoral dissertation, University of Kansas, 1970). D.A. 31A, No. 9, 4819–20.

[3]Arlette Zenatti. "Melodic Memory Tests; A Comparison of Normal Children and Mental Defectives." *Journal of Research in Music Education*, 23, No. 1 (Summer, 1975), pp. 41–52.

[4]Lee Knolle. "Sioux City's Special Brass Band; An Instrumental Program for the Mentally Retarded." *Music Educators Journal*, 59, No. 2 (October, 1973), pp. 47–48.

[5]Paul E. Rosene. "Music for EMH Children." *Music Educators Journal*, 67, No. 9 (May, 1981), p. 57.

[6]Sir Cyril Burt. *The Backward Child*, cited in Juliette Alvin, *Music for the Handicapped Child*, second edition. London: Oxford University Press, 1976, p. 68.

[7]Betsy Ann Larson. "A Comparison of Singing Ranges of Mentally Retarded and Normal Children with Published Songbooks Used in Singing Activities." *Journal of Music Therapy*, 14, No. 3 (Fall, 1977), pp. 139–43.

[8]Ruth Zinar. "Music in the Mainstream." *Teacher*, 96, No. 7 (March, 1978), p. 7.

[9]Wanda Bea Lathom. "Retarded Children's Retention of Songs, Stories and Poems." (Unpublished doctoral dissertation. University of Kansas, 1970.) Dissertation Abstracts, 31A, No. 9, pp. 4819–20.

[10]Linda Louise Kelly. "A Combined Experimental and Descriptive Study on the Effect of Music on Reading and Language." (Unpublished doctoral dissertation, University of Pennsylvania, 1981.)

[11]Diana Nicholson. "Music as an Aid to Learning." (Unpublished doctoral dissertation, New York University, 1972.)

[12]Esther Seides. "The Effect of Talent Class Placement of Slow Learners in the Seventh Grade of a New York City Junior High School." (Unpublished doctoral dissertation, New York University, 1967.)

[13]Michael Gordon. "The Effect of Contingent Music Instruction on the Language Reading Behavior and Musical Performance Ability of Middle School Students." (Unpublished doctoral dissertation, Teachers College, Columbia University, 1977.)

[14]Laura Gilbert Dorow. "Televised Music Lessons as Educational Reinforcement for Correct Mathematical Responses with the Educable Mentally Retarded." *Journal of Music Therapy*, 13, No. 2 (Summer, 1976), pp. 76–86.

[15]Cornelia Yarbrough, Margaret Charboneau, and Joel Wapnick. "Music as Reinforcement for Correct Mathematics and Attending in Ability Assigned Mathematics Classes." *Journal of Music Therapy*, 14, No. 2 (Summer, 1977), pp. 77–88.

[16]Letter, *Woman's Day*, November 15, 1983, p. 4.

[17]Letter, *Family Circle*, May 8, 1984, p. 10.

[18]Katherine Moran. Student Field Work Log. York College of the City University of New York, March 22, 1983.

[19]Barbara Force. "The Effects of Mainstreaming on the Learning of Nonretarded Children in an Elementary Music Classroom." *Journal of Music Therapy*, 20, No. 1 (Spring, 1983), pp. 2–13.

[20]Ruth Zinar. *Music in Your Classroom*. West Nyack, New York: Parker Publishing Company, Inc., 1983, p. 165.

C H A P T E R ✗ 6

MUSIC FOR THE
HEARING-IMPAIRED CHILD

"Music for the deaf" may seem to be a contradiction in terms, but actually it existed as long ago as 1802. Since then, it has been employed as an aid in teaching other subjects as well as for its aesthetic values. One of the earliest articles dealing with the values of music study for the deaf appeared in 1848 in *American Annals of the Deaf and Dumb*,[1] and many reports dating from the early 1900s and before tell of military bands and schools for the deaf and of the incorporation of music into the curriculum of these schools. Playing instruments, engaging in body rhythms, sensing string instruments, and participating in marching bands were all part of the curriculum for the hearing-impaired. Another early use of music for these children was at the Central Institute for the Deaf in St. Louis, Missouri, established in 1914. There, they "used piano, accordion, harmonium and similar musical instruments, being especially interested in those that gave opportunity for combined tactile and auditory impressions."[2]

Today, with the development of electronic equipment and the improvement of hearing aids and other scientific advances, more activities and experiences in music are possible than ever before. For example, at the Lexington School for the Deaf in Queens, New York, classes for deaf children in modern ballet and jazz dancing are held and the pupils give frequent public performances.[3] At the J.C. Ammanschool voor doven in Amsterdam, the children play recorders and resonator bells and learn to dance and pantomime to music.[4] At the Millridge Center for Hearing Impaired in Ohio, the profoundly and severely hearing-impaired pupils chant songs as they gesture and mime and they play recorders and resonator bells in musical ensembles.[5]

In the Edgemont, New York school district, several deaf children eager to join the band were successfully taught to play instruments. Learning to read notes and to use the correct fingering and rhythms presented no problems for them. Not only did their skills become equal to those of the hearing children, but psychological values of achievement and participation with others were called "immeasurable."[6]

Hearing loss can be caused by an obstruction which prevents sound waves from reaching the brain or it can be neural in origin. Damage of one type or another can be congenital or result from disease, medication, or accident. When mainstreaming became law, some five percent of special pupils (about 302,000) were labelled "hard of hearing" and about 45,000 of them deaf.[7] It is quite probable that as time goes by, hearing impairments may become more prevalent because of "noise pollution"—low-flying jet planes, amplified "rock" music, exposure in cities to screeching subway trains, factory noises, etc. In addition, the adolescent fad of walking through streets and listening through earphones to radios with the volume turned up so loud that passersby can hear the sound will undoubtedly result in a higher proportion of young people with damaged hearing.

Decibels (db.) measure the degree of loudness of a sound; the softest possible "threshold of sound" that can be heard by the average human ear being zero decibels. At one hundred twenty db., there is discomfort and at one hundred thirty to forty, the threshold of pain with possible damage to the ear is reached. In between there is a whole scale of measurements: a pin dropping, ten to twenty db.; a quiet voice, thirty db.; the normal speaking voice, fifty db.; shouting, eighty db.; a baby shrieking into its mother's ear, one hundred seventeen db.; an airplane close by or amplified "rock" music at six feet, one hundred twenty db.

A person with normal hearing can easily distinguish sounds between ten and one hundred twenty decibels. Mild hearing loss means that the individual can hear normal speech but not sounds softer than thirty to forty decibels. Hearing aids are recommended for those with moderate hearing loss (unable to hear below fifty to seventy decibels). For those with severe loss, sounds below seventy to eighty-five decibels cannot be heard but if the sounds are louder than that, they can distinguish pitch and intensity in music and tell whether a violin or flute is being played.

The majority of those diagnosed as hearing-impaired have profound loss; they cannot hear below the eighty-five to one hundred ten db. range.[8] For them, hearing aids may not be sufficient and therefore they need to learn to lip-read and/or use sign language. But even with this profound degree of impairment, they can still hear the loudest levels of music and are able to tell the difference between a sustained and percussive sound.

The totally deaf—a little more than ten percent of the hearing-impaired—can only experience sound as vibrations felt through the skin, bones, and head cavities. A hearing-impaired person is considered deaf when hearing "is nonfunctional for the ordinary purposes of life."[9] If able to function aurally either with or without a hearing device, he is considered to be hard of hearing.

The development in 1984 of the cochlear implant (an electronic inner ear that stimulates the auditory nerve) has enabled some totally deaf people to distinguish sounds, such as door bells and automobile horns, for the first time. Although they cannot distinguish words with the cochlear implant, they can hear music and voices to some extent. One of the earliest recipients of a cochlear implant said of her new hearing world, "I don't like rock or hard music because I can't hear rhythm. . . . I prefer mellow music because it is easy on the ear."[10]

Thus, we can see that even with a minimal amount of hearing, there is an aesthetic response and preferences are expressed. Those hearing-impaired who can be helped to hear by using hearing aids have still broader opportunities for true musical experiences.

CHARACTERISTICS OF THE HEARING-IMPAIRED

Hearing impairment acts as a barrier to social contact. Unless this feeling of isolation is countered by experiences of communicating and participating with others, some form of maladjustment—poorly controlled emotions, inflexibility, egocentricity, withdrawal, or depression—can result.

For a school child, hearing impairment can affect the learning process and lead to a shorter than average memory of auditory stimulus. Because he cannot hear the teacher's instructions, the deaf or hard of hearing child can find himself getting into trouble. And sometimes, because of the lack of speech or slow developing in the understanding of speech, a hearing-impaired child has mistakenly been thought to be retarded. Sometimes a hearing-impaired child is awkward and tense or has a clumsy gait, walking with a shuffle and with shoulders bent.

Communication—whether through sign language, lip-reading, gesture, facial expression, finger spelling, demonstrations, or speech —is a prime necessity for the hearing-impaired. Some schools for the deaf have stressed lip-reading while others incorporate signing, but the American Council of Educators of the Deaf believes in "total communication"—any form of communication that will help to cut through the isolation. Fortunately, electronic hearing aids have made a positive contribution to the lives and education of the hearing-impaired.

MUSICAL CHARACTERISTICS OF THE HEARING-IMPAIRED

There is some disagreement about whether the deaf can appreciate music aesthetically and emotionally. Juliette Alvin, an eminent music therapist, believes that music cannot be an aesthetic experience for them because they cannot distinguish tone color and harmony, intervals, and the full range of pitch.[11] However, when deaf children expressed their reactions to concert goings, they were filled with enthusiasm, saying things like, "It felt like waves hitting you"; "The music sounded like waves"; "The sounds were beautiful."[12] Sensing vibrations of the music apparently provides a different type of beauty.

A deaf student percussionist explains, "A person does not have to hear music in order to enjoy, appreciate, and perform it. . . . Music can provide a feeling of achievement, give personal pleasure as well as pleasure to other people, and in general, furnish an individual with a way to express herself. For these reasons, I want to continue taking part in soundless musical activities."[13]

The totally deaf can enjoy learning to play instruments, and through sensing vibrations, they can dance and engage in movement activities. The hard of hearing can have still more musical experiences than this; those with impairments up to moderate and severe levels are able to participate in many musical activities. They may "even excel in rhythmic activities."[14] The reasons for this are several. Firstly, the hearing-impaired can hear more frequencies in music (i.e., they can hear a wider range of pitches) than they can in speech. Secondly, most instruments are louder than speech. In addition, with the use of hearing aids, the hard of hearing are able to experience more of the sounds of music.

Some studies have revealed previously unsuspected musical abilities in the hearing-impaired. For example, rhythmic responsiveness of thirty-one profoundly or severely hearing-impaired pupils wearing hearing aids was compared to that of an equal number of normal hearing pupils. Meter recognition and awareness of beat, tempo, and tempo changes were tested. Not only were the hearing-impaired able to recognize rhythms, but they had higher scores than the normal pupils in aspects such as maintaining a steady beat and feeling metric accents.[15] There are problems in duplicating rhythms of *melodies*,[16] but when hearing and deaf children in the third grade were asked to duplicate rhythms played on a drum, the deaf children made fewer errors in beat and rhythm patterns than the youngsters with normal hearing.[17] At the start, they did not do as well, but with practice, even as the examples became more difficult, their performances improved. This was because their desire to do well increased their attentiveness; they began to count the beats they saw, duplicating visual stimuli with kinesthetic imitation.[18]

The ability of the hearing-impaired to maintain a beat over a period of time does appear to depend on the rate of speed of the beat. When fourth- and sixth-grade hearing-impaired youngsters were asked to follow metronome beats by playing on a wood block with a mallet and then to continue playing after the metronome was turned off, their response was best at eighty-eight beats per second, the closest to a child's pulse. This suggests that rhythm exercises should be presented originally at this tempo until accuracy is established.[19]

This underlying rhythmic ability pinpoints an essential part of the education of the hearing-impaired. Because communication for them must be largely through gesture, movement is a natural response.

The musical education of the deaf is usually neglected because it's taken for granted that it would not be of any value for them—in spite of the fact that some teachers of the profoundly hearing-impaired and deaf have found some of them to be talented musically.[20] However, music and rhythmic activities not only aid in body control but also in speech development, word accents, and enunciation. (At the Metropolitan School for the Deaf in Toronto, the program combines speech and speech rhythms with movement and singing.)[21]

A. van Uden, a world authority on teaching the deaf, has stated: "Deaf children have a great and basic need for a total rhythmic education from childhood, the method of which must use sound perception to its full extent. . . . Music and dance continuously train the auditory and vibratory senso-motoric functions as such . . . intense training in rhythm of the whole body, of breathing and speech, integrated with sound perception . . . is a must in schools for the deaf."[22]

Given the opportunity to have movement and music experiences, the responses of the deaf and hearing-impaired are excellent.

MUSIC ACTIVITIES

In teaching music to the hearing-impaired, "it is the[ir] abilities and not . . . disabilities . . . which must be cultivated."[23] The abilities to feel and respond to rhythms, to make maximum use of any residual hearing, and to develop sensitivity to the vibrations resulting from sound are those which have the most significance for music education.

A hearing-impaired child must learn the optimum use of a hearing aid, and for this, an educational process is needed. He or she must also learn to overcome the initial reluctance to wear an aid that so many hearing-impaired people have. The child should not be allowed to set his/her own hearing aid because he/she may make it too loud and cause additional hearing loss from excessively high sound levels. Instead, the degree of loudness at which an aid should be set ought to be determined by a qualified specialist. With the proper adjustments, most hard of hearing children will be able to hear and participate in a goodly number of music activities. If the impairments, however, are due to neural hearing problems, there will be some distortion of sounds.

Because there is the danger that sounds which are too loud can reach the threshold of pain, it is important *not to set* the volume control for recorded music *loud enough for the child to hear the softest sounds*. If this is not done, when some loud tones are reached, they might be beyond the threshold of pain. Setting the hearing aid so that just the moderate level of tones can be heard is best for listening activities. The same thing holds true when a child is experimenting with playing a drum or cymbals; either the hearing aid should be shut off or the instrument should be held away from the ear. The aid should also be turned down when the child participates in *group* activities, such as singing or playing of rhythm instruments.

Usually, the tones that are best amplified by a hearing aid are those between middle C and three octaves above. This enables the children to experience a much larger range of tones. Because a hearing aid picks up all sounds and because it picks up best those closest to it, the hearing-impaired child should sit close to the desired source of sound.

Once the children's hearing aids are adjusted, there are a number of things that you can do to facilitate all areas of learning for the hearing-impaired, as follows:

1. Sit facing the children so that they can derive additional meaning from your facial expressions and from lip reading. As you speak, enunciate carefully, synchronizing gestures and actions with the movements of your lips.

2. While sign language is helpful, it is not necessary. Much can be communicated through gesture, lip reading, and pantomime.

3. Eye contact is very important. For that reason, use the overhead projector instead of a chalkboard as much as possible so that you face the class more often.

4. Speak in a low-pitched voice (that is, "low" as compared to "high" pitched tones, not as compared to "loud" tones) because the hearing-impaired hear low-frequency sounds best.

5. There is some disagreement among experts as to whether music activities should be conducted in rooms with wooden floors. They do transmit sounds and vibrations best, but because the deaf and profoundly hearing-impaired will have to function in many types of environments, they cannot always rely on vibrations felt through the floor. For this reason, some teachers who specialize in teaching the deaf prefer to train them to sense air vibrations.[24]

Basically, there are the following four approaches to teaching music activities to the hearing-impaired: visual stimuli, movement, vibration, and the use of hearing aids.

Developing Sensitivity to Vibrations

In order for the hearing-impaired to apprehend music as much as possible, the development of sensitivity to sound vibrations is essential. A number of activities can aid in this:

1. Have the children lie on a wooden floor as music is played so that the vibrations can be felt through the whole body.

2. Have several children stand with their bodies touching a piano as they watch the pianist. In this way, they can feel the difference in their bodies when they see the performer playing or stopping. Then, they can stand with their backs to the piano, relying solely on air vibrations to determine whether or not the pianist is playing.

3. The children can also touch the piano with their hands, then gradually move away, always indicating whether they are aware of the music starting and stopping. Later, as the pianist plays in different tempos, they can try to walk around the piano, starting and stopping with the music.

4. Concepts of high and low pitch can be taught by having the children feel the sounding board of the piano, sensing with their fingers the differences in vibrations of various pitch levels.

5. Open the piano and let the children see the difference between the thinner, shorter strings for the high tones and the thicker, heavier strings for the low tones.

6. Make cards labelled "High" and "Low" and place them on the keyboard so that the children can learn to associate the vibrations with the position on the keyboard. After a while, they can try to guess whether a sound is high or low just from feeling the vibrations.

7. Have the children touch a drum as it is played and have them count the beats. Then they can try to sense the indirect vibrations by touching the table or floor on which the drum is placed. Finally, have them stand near the instrument and try to count the number of beats by sensing sound through air vibrations.

Listening Activities

As previously indicated, the hearing-impaired can listen to recorded music using hearing aids adjusted to the proper degree of loudness. This means that very soft sounds may not be heard but this is necessary to avoid a painful degree of loudness. When hard of hearing children listened to music using earphones and had the opportunity to hear music at various decibels from sixty to ninety (or to turn the music off if they wished), most of them preferred an intensity in the eighty to ninety decibel range. At this level, there was less hyperactivity and the children showed much pleasure, smiling and laughing. Some of them selected other levels of intensity, so this has to be worked out on an individual basis.[25]

In addition to listening to recordings, other attractive activities can enhance listening experiences, such as:

1. Give the hearing-impaired children the opportunity to attend live performances together with the other children. The added visual stimulus of seeing the musicians will increase the children's interest and attention.

2. At concerts, if possible, have them sit near those instruments —double bass, tuba, trombone, etc.—that would enable them to take advantage of their ability to sense best lower-pitched instruments.

3. Similarly, if you play the piano, have the hearing-impaired children sit near your left hand (near the lower-pitched tones).

4. Put paper on top of a speaker box as a recording is played and let the children finger paint to the music. If deaf, the children will be responding creatively to the vibrations of the music, and the hard of hearing will have the dual stimuli of sound and touch.

5. To alleviate the difficulty in telling the source of a sound, play a drum and have the children listen with their eyes closed. In trying to hear and point to the direction from which the sounds are coming, they will be sharpening their auditory abilities.

6. Provide large charts showing diagrams of the themes of the music they are listening to. They may not be able to hear the details of the music, but the visuals help to give the general idea.

Rhythm and Movement Activities

Movement activities are essential for the hearing-impaired to help develop ease of body coordination. Whether the child can hear a rhythm or not, *he can still feel it.* After all, rhythm notation is, to a large extent, the intellectualization through written symbols of many of the natural rhythms we feel inside ourselves. Through modalities of sight, movement and touch, rhythm concepts and notation can be taught and experienced. Remember that it is not necessary to hear in order to feel or beat a rhythm. The child can see others perform the rhythm and then be able to reproduce it kines-thetically. The following are some activities that you can use:

1. Always demonstrate the movements you want the child to perform.

2. Give the hearing-impaired children a chance to perform both as soloists and as part of the group to enhance feelings of participation and improved self-image.

3. Play a pattern of short and long sustained tones on an electronic organ as the children watch. Repeat the same rhythm pattern and then demonstrate how to beat the pattern. Now play it again and have the children, with eyes shut, beat the same pattern.

4. Play a sustained tone on an electronic organ (a good instrument for these activities because of its resonance). Have the children move their arms while the tone lasts and indicate with an abrupt gesture when the music stops. The same thing can be done using scarves, moving them through the air as long as the tone sounds.

5. Using exaggerated movements, clap, conduct, or play a steady beat on a drum. Have the deaf children watch you and respond by clapping or conducting with you or making believe they are playing drums. When the beat is established, have them "mark time" in place and then march to the beat.

6. Tap a steady beat on the child's hand and then have him respond by tapping, clapping, and then walking to the beat. Explain that the movement or duration of that "walking" beat is called a quarter note ($\quarternote$). Do the same thing when teaching eighth notes ($\eighthnotes$), etc.

7. Tap a steady rhythm pattern in $\frac{2}{4}$, $\frac{3}{4}$, or $\frac{4}{4}$ meter on the child's hand, making the first beat of each measure stronger. The child will feel the stronger first beat on his hand. Have him try to clap the meter, using more strength on the first beat.

8. Conduct a $\frac{2}{4}$, $\frac{3}{4}$, or $\frac{4}{4}$ meter, exaggerating the emphasis on the first beat, and have the children respond by tapping, clapping, or playing on drums the meter they see conducted. Have them use more strength on the first beat.

9. Have the children listen to music using earphones, instructing them to respond freely with arm movements to the rhythms they hear and/or sense through vibrations.

10. Exaggerating your movements, play a short rhythmic pattern on a low-pitched drum as the children watch carefully and then imitate you. Start with simple, short rhythms and gradually make them more difficult.

11. Have the children stand close to you, with their backs turned as you play a short rhythm pattern on a low-pitched drum. Have them try to imitate the rhythm by clapping or playing a drum.

12. Go through several steps to teach a dance. First, demonstrate the dance. Set the beat and have the children clap the rhythm. Then teach the steps. If a record is used, have the hearing-impaired child touch the speaker to feel the beat. Pair a deaf child with either a hearing or hearing-impaired child who is familiar with the dance and have them dance together. If a wooden floor is used (with deaf children), the vibrations of the music will be felt more strongly and the children should be able to participate readily with the others. The hard of hearing should be encouraged to sense as much of the music as they can using their hearing aids and sensitivity to air vibrations.

13. On occasion, have the hearing-impaired children move and dance in front of a mirror to help them develop ease of movement.

All of these movement activities can be of value for all children. With them, the hearing-impaired children can have the same opportunity to move creatively and freely to music, whether they are responding to sounds heard through hearing aids or to vibrations.

Playing Instruments

Rhythm instruments do not present a real problem for the hearing-impaired when they can easily follow your beat and watch their classmates to learn simple rhythm patterns. However, certain instruments are preferable. Wood blocks, tone blocks and rhythm sticks, for example, have poor vibrations, while a pancake drum (which can be held close to the body), low-pitched drums, or the tambourine have excellent resonance. The high pitch of triangles and finger cymbals makes them less useful as a choice for the hearing-impaired. Wrapping a child's legs around a bongo drum while playing it can be another enjoyable activity. If the activity's goal is to increase sensitivity to auditory stimuli rather than vibratory stimuli, then have the child keep the instrument away from his ear and use an instrument in a low register.

For the deaf child, have him hold the autoharp in his lap as he plays it so that he can feel the vibrations, or else it can be placed on the floor with his ear touching the instrument.

As music, classroom, or special education teacher, you may find some hearing-impaired children eager to join the band or orchestra, or parents may come to you for advice regarding lessons. In these cases, the attributes of both child and instrument need to be considered.

Among the string instruments, harp and guitar are suitable—the harp because the strings are close to the ear and the guitar because of the body contact in playing. On the other hand, because of intonation problems in playing the violin and cello and because there are no indications to show the child where to place his fingers, success is less likely with these instruments.

The clarinet and saxophone are the wind instruments that have been most successfully used with the hearing-impaired. This is because they have definite fingering, good resonance, and a large frequency range. The clarinet is a good choice because the players can "feel the vibrations of the clarinet both on their lips and in their chest cavities" and they are "thusly stimulated to sing or hum the same melodies" they play.[26]

While brass instruments have been successfully taught, they present some difficulties—the French horn and trombone especially requiring a good sense of pitch. In the Edgemont, New York school district, the profoundly deaf children who joined the band class learned to play trumpet, clarinet, and flute and participated in performances. This they accomplished through observing the other children who played the same instruments, touching the other instruments to get the beat, and watching the conductor.[27]

Good results have also been achieved with electronic piano "lab" instruction because the instruments have sustained tones and resonance and the pupils wear hearing aids.

Unfortunately, recorders, melody flutes, tonettes, and flutophones —the classroom wind instruments—are not very suitable for deaf and profoundly hearing-impaired pupils because they are so high pitched, have little resonance, and will squeak if blown too hard. A much better choice for these children is the "Melodica," an easily learned wind instrument that is played by blowing into a mouthpiece while fingering the keys which are arranged to look like a piano keyboard. The instrument has much more resonance than the recorder or melody flute and it is held close to the face. Hearing-impaired children can participate in classroom instrumental ensembles by playing the autoharp, rhythm instruments, melodica, or resonator bells. When you have rhythm band or other instrumental work, let the hearing-impaired child have a "buddy" to help or show him what to do if problems arise.

Singing with Hearing-Impaired Children

There are differences of opinion among music teachers who specialize in teaching the deaf as to whether they can or should be taught to sing. Not all attempt this, feeling that movement, listening, and instrumental activities should be stressed. It is only to be expected that there would be a great variation in the ability of hearing-impaired children to learn to sing. This would depend on the degree of hearing loss, on the extent to which a hearing aid can help, and on how much singing experience th₂ children have had. Some can achieve chanting in rhythm, some can "move" their voices in the general direction of the pitch, and some can (more or less frequently) sing the correct tones. Teaching the profoundly hearing-impaired and deaf to sing on pitch is a long process that can take up to five years of instruction, and even then success is uncertain.

Although some may never be able to sing on pitch, the opportunity to participate with others helps them to feel part of the group and aids in breath control and speech development.

The natural speaking voice of seriously hearing-impaired children is either a monotone (usually around middle C) or else limited to quite a small range. The same thing is true of their singing range, but this limited range can be extended gradually. Playing the kazoo has been found to be of value in this regard.

Strangely enough, some who are seriously hearing-impaired will sing harmonizing tones, perhaps connected in some way to their sensing vibrations of "overtones" (in acoustics, higher tones which sound at the same time as a lower one to make up a musical tone).

In choosing songs for the hearing-impaired, try to stay within a limited range (from middle C to the octave above) because these tones are close to the children's natural pitch range and are among those best amplified by hearing aids. Use songs that have *natural* speech accents, with the stress of the music falling on the word syllables that would normally be emphasized. Action songs help the children learn the words more easily.

When teaching a song, have the children sit near you, watching your face as you sing. This helps lip reading and aids in understanding the song better. To help develop a singing tone, you can try the following steps:

- Sing B flat below middle C and have the child feel your face or place his cheek against yours to feel the vibrations. Then, after having the child feel your Adam's apple as you sing the tone, he can try to reproduce the sound.
- Now sing the B flat an octave higher, repeating the process. The child will be able to sense the rise and fall of pitch as vibrations in the Adam's apple. Little by little, tones closer together can be tried.

When teaching a song, have the words written out on a chart and illustrate new words with pictures or actions wherever possible. Teach the words and rhythm first and then some pitch levels. Then add mime, gesture, or signing. (Some teachers find that signing from the start takes too much attention away from the singing.) As the children sing, cue them by mouthing the words, pointing to the words on the chart, and using gestures to indicate the rise and fall of pitch or the rhythms.

There have been some highly successful singing programs with hearing-impaired children. One, the "Total Communication Choir" in the tri-city area of Michigan, included normal hearing and hearing-impaired children with losses ranging from moderate to profound. All the children were given copies of the songs with both words and signs indicated. The rhythm was taught first and then all the children practiced chanting and signing in rhythm. After this, a simple accompaniment was played, with hearing children and teachers singing. Finally, the hearing-impaired children joined in and they all sang together. According to the teachers, "Improved communication between hearing and hearing-impaired students [was] a noticeable benefit."[28]

In another program at P.S. 47, New York City's School for the Deaf, singing activities were centered around the guitar, using folk songs and special teacher-written songs, repetitive in nature and simplified to make performance easier.[29] In this endeavor, which took place in the 1960's, the guitar was selected as the accompanying instrument because the teacher could sit facing the children while they could sit close enough to her to lip-read. They could also see the rhythm strums and were able to reach out with their hands to feel the vibrations of the guitar. (If you cannot play the guitar, the easily mastered autoharp would have all these same advantages.)

Today, there are many exemplary singing programs (including one at P.S. 47). Of course, the deaf and hearing-impaired pupils will not always sing on pitch, but the enjoyment that they derive from participating with the other children more than makes up for any resulting dissonance.

Music As an Aid to Speech

The rhythms of music used in movement, chanting, and instrument activities can help to counteract the monotony of speech of deaf children and those with a moderately severe to profound range of hearing loss. This is done by using many possible ways of coordinating the meter and musical accent of words, spoken phrases, the child's own body movements and the sensory perception of vibrations.

Starting with one and then two-syllable words, their rhythms can be illustrated in a number of ways. For example, if two-syllable words such as Su - san, mo - ther, ba - by, mar - ket (i.e., / — / — / — / —) are being taught, the child needs to know where to place the accent. You can do the following:

1. Have the child place his hand on a drum and watch your lips as you say the words and beat the drum ($\frac{2}{4}$ ♩ ♩). The child will feel the stronger beat through the drum variations at the same time that he is reading your lips. In this way, he can see how the words are formed.

2. Say the word as you tap the child's hand with your own, emphasizing the first syllable by tapping harder for it.

3. Have the child watch your face as you say the word and have him clap, tap, or stamp its rhythm using more strength on the first syllable. Then have him try to say the word with correct emphasis.

4. Have the child play the rhythm of the word on a drum, emphasizing the first syllable. Then say the word as he plays.

5. Have the child, his hand touching the piano, feel its vibrations and watch your lips as you say the words and simultaneously play chords.

6. Have the child analyze the word rhythms he feels tapped on his hand, he sees played on the drum or piano, or he moves to by clapping, stamping, etc. Ask him how many syllables he notices and which one is louder.

The same procedures can be used for three-syllable words, short phrases, and later, for choral speaking.

To develop flowing (correctly accented speech), start with short phrases and go through the following steps:

Say the words to a rhythm pattern as the children watch you and lip-read (e.g., My, but it's hot outside.)

Place the words on the board.

Demonstrate the rhythm on a drum.

Have the children imitate the rhythm on drums and other instruments.

Have the children speak the sentence as they beat the rhythm.

For choral speaking, start by teaching the rhythm patterns first, a brief section at a time, and then when the children can remember and clap the rhythms, teach the words.

Perhaps the best way to develop pitch variety in the voices of the hearing-impaired is through singing activity. Then, when the child can feel the differences in pitch vibrations in his own body and knows what "up" and "down" mean, he can be helped to learn when to raise or lower the pitch of his speaking voice.

Deaf and hard of hearing children can join in most music games even if their hearing is not acute enough with hearing aids to participate in exactly the same way as the rest of the class. For example, in one activity, to develop the sense of pitch, you can distribute at random Swiss bells (hand-held ringing bells) of varying pitches to a number of children and select a child to be "It." "It" keeps rearranging the children holding the bells until they are in the correct order to play a scale. The hearing-impaired child may not be able to distinguish the delicate high tones, but he can participate by being one of the children holding a bell. The same sort of adaptation can be made in similar group activities.

Other activities for improvement of self-image for the hearing-impaired are "body parts" songs and "name songs." The use of relaxation exercises to sedative music helps to reduce tension.

You would not say to an awkward child, "Don't dance. Just sit and watch the other children," nor would you say to a nonathletic child, "You're not good at throwing and catching a ball and you don't know how to swim. So don't play games with the other children and stay out of the water." Nor should a hearing-impaired child be deprived of music.

The studies described in this chapter and the experiences of those who have taught the deaf and hard of hearing prove that they can learn music and participate in singing, moving to music, and playing musical instruments.

By making maximum use of their residual hearing and the ability to learn to sense air vibrations, they can be helped to have more ease of movement and more flowing speech patterns. Most of all, the sense of isolation can be diminished as they develop relationships with others through music.

SUMMARY

Music was used in schools for the deaf almost two hundred years ago, and today hearing-impaired children learn to dance to music, play musical instruments, sing and, to some extent, listen to music.

The degree of hearing loss ranges from mild to profound to total deafness, with the majority of the hearing-impaired having profound loss. With the use of hearing aids, even those with profound loss can hear the loudest levels of music and tell whether a tone is sustained. Those with less severe impairment can recognize melody and tone quality of instruments.

Because the deaf and hearing-impaired frequently suffer from a sense of isolation, joining others in music activities can help them overcome their feelings of being shut off from their peers. By using residual hearing and developing a higher degree of sensitivity to air vibrations through step-by-step procedures, they can participate in many satisfying music experiences.

Learning to play rhythm instruments by watching the teacher and classmates is comparatively simple. (Studies indicate that deaf children can imitate drumbeats better than those with normal hearing.) They do not have to hear the sounds to appreciate the rhythmic movements. Those who wish to learn an instrument of band or orchestra should select one that has good resonance with medium to low pitch and that requires the fingers to be held in fixed position or with positions for fingers marked (e.g., guitar rather than violin, clarinet rather than French horn or flute).

Dancing and movement activities can be learned by sensing air vibrations or vibrations from a wooden floor and by observing others. Pleasure at concerts is enhanced by sitting near low-pitched instruments.

One of the most important roles of music for the deaf is helping them speak smoothly, with variation in voice pitch and proper word emphasis. This is done through a number of movement and instrumental activities related to word accents and rhythms.

NOTES

[1]Eleanor M. Edwards. *Music Education for the Deaf.* South Waterford, Maine: The Merriam-Eddy Company, 1974, p. 2.

[2]Ruth Bender. *The Conquest of Defense.* Cleveland: The Press of Case Western Reserve University, 1970, p. 172.

[3]On August 5, 1985, the dance group of Lexington School for the Deaf performed at the International Symposium on Music; Rehabilitation and Well-Being, held at Goldwater Memorial Hospital in New York City.

[4]Ben Gerits. "Music for the Hearing Impaired." International Symposium on Music; Rehabilitation and Human Well-Being, August 5, 1985.

[5]Marilyn Landis. "I Am a Promise." International Symposium on Music, August 6, 1985.

[6]Melvin Folts. "Deaf Children Cannot Play a Musical Instrument Can They?" *New York State School Music News*, 39, No. 4 (December, 1976), pp. 34-5.

[7]Richard M. Graham. "Seven Million Plus Need Special Attention; Who Are They" in *Music in Special Education.* Washington, D.C.: Music Educators National Conference, 1972, p. 7.

[8]Hayes A. Newly. *Audiology.* New York: Appleton-Century-Crofts, 1972, p. 307.

[9]Ibid., p. 306.

[10]*New York Times*, November 30, 1984. A1, p. 1.

[11]Juliette Alvin. *Music for the Handicapped Child*, second edition. London: Oxford University Press, 1976, p. 136.

[12]John Grayson, "A Playground of Musical Sculpture," in *Music in Special Education*, p. 35.

[13]Carol Epley. "In a Soundless World of Musical Enjoyment," in *Music in Special Education*, p. 39.

[14]Richard M. Graham and Alice S. Beer. *Teaching Music to the Exceptional Child.* Englewood Cliffs, New Jersey: Prentice-Hall, Inc., 1980, p. 60.

[15]Alice-Ann Darrow. "The Beat Reproduction Response of Subjects with Normal and Impaired Hearing: An Empirical Comparison." *Journal of Music Therapy*, 16, No. 2 (Summer, 1979), pp. 91-8.

[16]Darrow. "A Comparison of Rhythmic Responsiveness in Normal and Hearing Impaired Children and an Investigation of the Relationship of Rhythmic Responsiveness to the Suprasegmental Aspects of Speech Perception." *Journal of Music Therapy*, 21, No. 2 (Summer, 1984), pp. 48–66.

[17]Olga Korduba. "Duplicated Rhythmic Patterns Between Deaf and Normal Hearing Children." *Journal of Music Therapy*, 12, No. 3 (Fall, 1975), pp. 136–46.

[18]Ibid.

[19]Darrow. "The Beat Reproduction Response. . . ."

[20]Marilyn Landis. "I Am a Promise."

[21]Joan Fahey and Lois Birkenshaw. "Bypassing the Ear; The Perception of Music by Feeling and Touch," in *Music in Special Education*, pp. 28–33; 65–6.

[22]John Grayson. "A Playground of Musical Sculpture." p. 35 citing A. van Uden, *A World of Language for Deaf Children* (Netherlands: Rotterdam University Press, 1970) in *Music in Special Education.*

[23]Edwards. *Music Education for the Deaf*, p. 95.

[24]Gerits. "Music for the Hard of Hearing."

[25]Sally Baird. "A Technique to Assess the Preference for Intensity of Musical Stimuli in Young Hard of Hearing Children." *Journal of Music Therapy*, 6, No. 1 (Spring, 1969), pp. 6–11.

[26]*Music Education for the Deaf*, p. 60.

[27]"Deaf Children Cannot Play a Musical Instrument. . . ."

[28]Ruth Ann Knapp. "A Choir for Total Communication." *Music Educators Journal*, 66, No. 6 (February, 1980), pp. 54–5.

[29]Loretta Hogan, Patricia Bierne and Susan Butler. "A Music Program for Young Deaf Children." *The Volta Review*, 70, No. 7 (October, 1968), pp. 561–65.

CHAPTER ✗ 7

MUSIC FOR THE MOTOR-IMPAIRED CHILD

"A 'handicap' ceases to exist as a physical reality when it has been vanquished as a psychological reality."[1] Those music therapists who have seen extremely motor-handicapped children—permanently hospitalized, in wheelchairs with little or no use of arms and/or legs, with stunted growth and tracheotomies to allow excess fluid to be pumped from their lungs—smile when their names are sung, play rhythm instruments, and respond with pleasure to music activities, know the meaning of this statement.

As time goes by, more and more severely motor-impaired children can be found in the public schools. Mainstreaming laws account for this, as well as the fact that since the mid-1950's, newly devised prosthetics can aid the motor-impaired to participate in a number of activities.

Motor impairments can be caused by a large number and variety of things such as birth defects, accidents, diseases (e.g., muscular dystrophy, rheumatoid arthritis), skeletal deficiencies, weak muscles and joints, or amputation resulting from accident, infection, cancer, etc. Some motor-impaired children may be able to use their limbs to some extent while others may be confined to wheelchairs or have to use prosthetic devices. Despite their disabilities, they enjoy music as much as other children and have the same intellectual and emotional needs, including: independence, a feeling of achievement, and the opportunity to participate with others. They must also overcome any feelings of embarrassment resulting from their physical impairments and learn how to relax. Specific goals may be one or more of the fol-

141

lowing: hand–eye coordination, muscle strength, endurance, motor control, controlled lip closure, breath control, development of the ability to stretch muscles, visual coordination, or coordination of hand, eyes, and limbs.

How can music help towards the achievement of these manifold and varied results? A prescribed exercise may use specific muscle groups requiring the same specific movements used in playing a certain instrument. How much more fun it is for a child to bang on a drum than to move his forearm up and down forty-five times! Or, for children with strabismus (crossed eyes), to read piano music instead of doing eye exercises. Or for a child to play a clarinet rather than do breathing exercises. The reaching and stretching of fingers to play the piano can strengthen the muscles of the hand, while the use of a bow in playing the violin can strengthen the arm muscles.

There are numerous examples of motor-impaired pupils who have successfully learned to play musical instruments. Viewers of the television program "Who Are the De Bolts and Where Did They Get Nineteen Kids?" saw the unforgettable image of one of the De Bolt's foster children—born without arms or legs—joyfully playing a xylophone.[2] A music teacher tells of a child without fingers learning to play the French horn,[3] or (as in my own teaching experience) of the young girl, born with fingers growing from short stumps of arms, beautifully playing the recorder, autoharp, and melody bells. An outstanding program involving some four hundred children and adults, established at the Philadelphia Settlement Music School in cooperation with Moss Rehabilitation Hospital, uses instruction in musical instruments as an integral part of physical therapy.[4]

In still another special program at a hospital for motor-impaired children, every child, no matter how disabled, was able to make some contribution to musical productions.[5]

No matter how limited the participation may be, it is possible for motor-impaired children to make music in some way. In addition, music can help to alleviate some accompanying symptoms of various diseases. For example, in one study, twenty-five subjects who had gait problems resulting from neuromuscular disorders selected music and percussive sounds they preferred. Then as they listened, they would try to walk in time to the music. Little by little as their rhythmic control increased, the music was made softer and softer until it was faded out entirely. All those who participated improved "in rhythmic-even walking and/or consistency of walking speed."[6]

It has been found that stimulative music can help the performance of a child with spastic cerebral palsy to become more controlled but cause the athetoid child (one having continual slow movements, especially of the extremities) to have uncontrolled, jerky movements. On the other hand, sedative music spoils the spastic child's performance but helps the athetoid child.[7] Obviously, this can create problems, and it also brings to light the most important aspect of any music program involving the motor-handicapped: it is absolutely essential to consult with a qualified professional (physician, therapist, etc.) before selecting or adapting any musical instrument or exercise to use with them. With the correct choice of activity and, if necessary, suitable adaptations of instruments or activities, music can help to provide pleasure, motor stimulation, and exercise.

MUSIC ACTIVITIES

Motor-impaired children should be made to feel as much at ease as possible in a room that is made as safe as possible for them. If there are wheelchairs, make room for them. Regular chairs should be a comfortable size and they should be secured to avoid sliding. If lap tables are needed, they should also be provided. It is important to prepare the class ahead of time so that they can be at ease with the motor-impaired child and understand that physical inability to do certain things does not preclude achievement in other ways. Some of the children can be appointed "buddies" to help, where necessary, with wheelchair dancing or playing instruments. It may be necessary for you to help gently with movements.

Plan for various activities including music listening, playing instruments, singing, and rhythmic response. Sometimes, you may find that you have to adapt activities or instruments. In any event, the child should not be forced to participate but welcomed and invited to join noncompetitive activities.

Movement Activities

Movement activities should usually be done at a slow pace and should be gentle ones. Music can be used to accompany the exercises (those prescribed or approved by a physician or other qualified professional). The purpose of the activities may be to relax, stimulate, or strengthen specific muscles.

Here are some rhythmic exercises therapists have used to accomplish specific goals:[8]

1. To strengthen legs for walking: lying on back and making believe one is pedaling a bike (to march music in a moderate tempo).

2. To improve supination (the turning of forearm or hand so that the palm faces upward): playing the drum with a double-headed drumstick, alternating heads of the stick.

3. To strengthen arms: playing the drums or cymbals.

4. To develop arm movements: playing vertical hanging chimes or ringing Swiss bells.

5. To improve wrist and finger movement: playing the autoharp.

6. To strengthen and lift arms: marching to lively music, waving streamers.

7. To cross midline: holding out two pancake drums and letting the child strike them one at a time. Repeat this several times, each time changing the position in which you hold the drums —further apart, one higher or lower, etc.—so that the child gets exercise moving his arm from one side to the other. This exercise also aids in coordinating eye and arm movements.

8. To strengthen back of neck: tossing a large balloon into the air and watching it as it slowly descends, then repeating. (*Very* slow waltz music such as Brahms' "Waltz in A flat" for piano is fine for this.)

9. To improve lateral (side to side) movement of upper arms and shoulders: making believe one is holding and rocking a baby (to lullabye music).

10. To improve balance: walking on a wide board or waving scarves while turning to moderately slow music (e.g., "Flow Gently Sweet Afton," "Beautiful Dreamer").

11. To correct a shuffling gait: using very low boxes as stepping stones and stepping over each one (to moderately slow music such as "Never on a Sunday," or a Greek "Slow Hosopikos").

Some form of simple, adapted classroom movement activities can be suitable for the motor-handicapped depending on the type and degree of impairment. Here are some from which you can choose:

1. Have the children stand in a circle (or else, be seated in wheelchairs) and pass "jungle bells" to slow music.

2. Do gentle "mirror" exercises. As you face the class, move your arms and hands to slow music and have the children mirror your actions. Children in wheelchairs who have use of their arms can easily participate in this activity. Later, one of the children can be the leader while you can, if needed, gently help the child to make the correct movements.

3. Play music and let the children "hand dance," moving fingers and hands to express the rhythms and moods of the music.

4. Do "wheelchair dancing." If necessary, have a music partner move the wheelchair in time to the music. Square dance and round dance formations can be appropriate for this, but remember that the music must be played at a slower tempo when wheelchairs are involved.

5. Have the children listen to music, moving their arms as far apart as they can to loud sections and then bringing them close together for soft sounds. This aids lateral movement.

6. Have the children play at being puppets. Make believe that strings are attached to the arms, legs, and head. As the music plays (the "Funeral March of a Marionette" by Gounod is excellent for this), you can pretend you are moving various strings, exercising whatever body part of the child is desired.

7. Have the children lie on the floor, and to the music, try to move one part of the body at a time. Some may need help with this.

8. Have parades, including the children in wheelchairs. Again, a music partner can help push the wheelchairs in time and formation.

9. Use gesture songs to encourage movement and exercise of specific muscle groups. For example, the movements suggested for "Row, Row, Row Your Boat" (in the chapter on "Music for the Emotionally Disturbed Child" for the purpose of using up excess energy) can be used to strengthen arms.

Gestures for "The Damper" (an "elimination" song, the score for which can be found in Chapter 2) can be changed to emphasize arm movements and eliminate standing and sitting down; again, for children confined to wheelchairs. This is done by spreading the arms apart and bringing them together on the words "Just the same, just the same" as the children remain seated throughout.

Special movements to encourage the use of fingers and hands can be done with the folk song "Pick a Bale of Cotton":

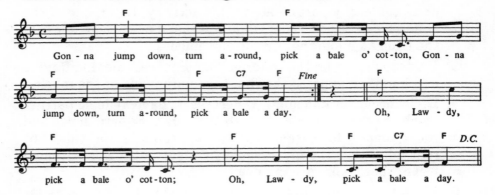

Gon - na jump down, turn a - round, pick a bale o' cot - ton, Gon - na

jump down, turn a - round, pick a bale a day.   Oh, Law - dy,

pick a bale o' cot - ton;   Oh, Law - dy, pick a bale a day.

Words	Motions
Gonna jump down,	Tap hands on table or lap desk.
Turn around,	Wind hands around each other.
Pick a bale o' cotton. . . .	Plucking movement with fingers.
Oh, Lawdy,	Clap hands on each syllable.
Pick a bale o' cotton, etc.	Plucking movements with fingers.

Zoltán Kodály was an eminent twentieth-century composer who developed a system of music education for his native Hungary. Included in this system are hand signals that indicate the tones of the scale, a different signal for each tone. The purpose of the signals was to develop the ability to sing melodies at sight. If you have the children practice singing these tones as they watch you and imitate your hand signals (see Figures 7-1 and 7-2), they will be exercising to develop wrist rotation.

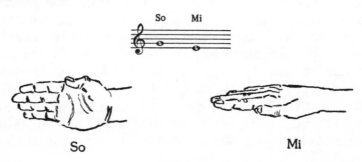

Figure 7-1

Extension and flexion of fingers can be encouraged by using the hand signals for these tones:

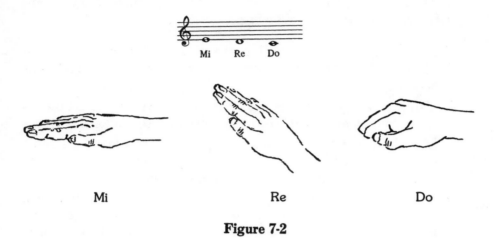

Figure 7-2

You can, after the children develop ease in following, singing, and signalling these tone groups, "mix" them; in this way, creating many simple attractive melodies. This type of activity can be fascinating for pupils of all ages.

For little children, finger-plays such as "Eency-Weency Spider" and "The Turtle" (both of these can be found in *Teacher's Guide to the Open Court Kindergarten Music Program*) can also provide valuable movements for hands, fingers, and arms.

All children can participate in movement activities in whatever way possible for them—swaying, waving arms, bending, rocking, etc. Those who are nonambulatory can move any way they can—rolling on the floor or nodding heads, moving facial muscles, etc. No one needs to feel "left out."

Playing Instruments

Because traditional instruments may not be suitable, sometimes a motor-impaired child will either need special adaptations to enable him to play, or he will be able to play them in an unorthodox fashion. Occasionally, a musical instrument may be selected specifically to alleviate a symptom. In addition, some special instruments have been created for children with various handicaps.[9]

ADAPTING INSTRUMENTS

Some of the simpler adaptations that you can make and that are in general use include the following:

1. For a child who has trouble grasping a drumstick, you can "thicken" the stick by wrapping carpet tape or foam rubber strips around it.

2. Using straps and cords, you can hang rhythm instruments from frames attached to wheelchairs and to walkers.

3. If a child has only one hand or if for some reason he can't cover the lower holes of a tonette, melody flute, or recorder to play simple melodies, use tape to cover these holes.

4. Sometimes fingers cannot hold a pick to strum the autoharp. In such instances, you can have the child use a "ring" pick, which is worn on the finger like a ring and is adjustable in size. These are available in music stores. You can also have the child use a tongue depressor wrapped with cloth or use a kitchen spatula with the handle removed.

5. If a child has poor muscle and hand–eye coordination, try putting a brightly colored mark on the bars of melody or resonator bells to help him "land" on the right spot.

6. Palm gloves can be used to hold drumsticks if the child is unable to bend his fingers. These look like gloves with the fingers removed and a loop sewn onto the palm through which a drumstick is inserted and then held in place.

7. If the child cannot hold them, jingle bells can be sewn onto bands or ribbons and tied around the youngster's wrist or ankle. He can then play by merely shaking his hand or foot.

8. For cerebral palsied children who have difficulty swinging a mallet from side to side, the bars of resonator bells can be placed in the order in which they will be played, rather than according to pitch.

9. Wrist straps can also be attached to cymbals for a child who can move arms laterally but cannot grasp the instruments.

Other, more complex adaptations have included attaching a violin or cello bow to an artificial arm and reversing the strings and bridge of the violin or cello so that fingering can be done with the right hand

and bowing with the left. A trumpet can be held in position by a special stand as the pupil uses one hand to depress the valves. Prosthetic devices that have hooks with rubber tips, which are made for arm amputees, have enabled pianists to play two-note chords. And special sticks that are individually made to meet an armless or paralyzed child's needs can be held in the mouth and used to play a percussion instrument.

ADAPTING THE METHOD OF PLAYING INSTRUMENTS

With flexibility and imagination, you will find that motor-impaired children can play rhythm and other instruments, ones that you initially might expect would present too many problems. For example:

1. A child with the use of only one arm can play the cymbals with a partner, with each child holding one cymbal. The same thing can be done with the tambourine, triangle, and tone block; one child holds the instrument, the other strikes it.

2. Conga-type drums don't require any stick at all and can be struck with an open hand. The tambourine doesn't require the player to lift his hand right after striking the instrument. Both of these instruments may be better than the drum for children without full use of arms or hands.

3. Hanging bells and chimes don't have to be rung or struck in the conventional way. Instead, they can be played using movements of elbows, arms, and feet—even movements of nose or chin.

4. Children with one arm can easily play such instruments as bells, tambourines, and drums, and there is a fairly large repertoire of one-hand music available for pianists.[10] A brass instrument for an amputee with a prosthesis can be held with the artificial arm, with the remaining hand doing the fingering.

5. Drums can be played using foot pedals, tambourines can be tapped on lap boards, maracas can be tied to a wrist or ankle or held between the chin and shoulder, and mallets of melody or resonator bells can be held between the teeth.

6. Try experimenting with simple, small electronic keyboards. Some of these are small and light enough to be played in bed, held in the lap, or placed on a lap board. Simple melodies can be played on them with settings for various pitch registers,

tone qualities, rhythm accompaniments and volumes. The advantages are not only the small size of the instruments and the variety of playing styles possible, but also that they take only the slightest pressure to play a tone. Hence, little finger strength or motion is required and playing can provide considerable fun and a feeling of accomplishment.

These are just a few suggestions for playing and adapting instruments with motor-impaired children. Look for additional ways to help pupils to participate with other children and to be part of a group instrumental ensemble.

SELECTING THE OPTIMUM INSTRUMENTS

Although teaching the instruments of the band and orchestra is the responsibility of the music specialist, the classroom and special education teacher should be aware, especially if consulted by parents or an eager child, of some of the values of instrumental lessons in alleviating certain symptoms.

As part of the work of the Philadelphia Settlement Music School, a book on the selection of musical instruments for the physically disabled was developed by music teachers together with therapists at Moss Rehabilitation Hospital.[11] This guide analyzes in precise detail the movements of the head, shoulders, elbows, forearms, wrists, thumbs, fingers and hands that are required to play a whole gamut of instruments. The information provided can help the music teacher, in consultation with a medical professional, to select the optimum instrument for a pupil with a particular disorder—one he would be able to play and/or one that can help to alleviate a specific symptom. Among the possible benefits of playing conventional instruments or simple musical toys are these:

1. Something as simple as giving a child a music box to play by winding the handle can help to develop arm and wrist rotation.
2. Playing rhythm instruments and resonator and song bells aids in developing grasping ability, control, and strength of arm movements.
3. Classroom wind instruments, such as a recorder or melody flute, can help to develop control of breath, swallowing, and mouth position.

4. Playing the piano develops muscle strength of fingers and hands and, especially when playing at the extreme ends of the keyboard, joint motion of shoulders. It aids in flexion (bending) at joints of fingers and thumbs, in extension and in coordination of fingers.

5. The violin exercises the arm and shoulder of the bow arm. (Joseph Fuchs, the violin virtuoso, used to tell how, as a child, he broke his arm when he fell off a table. It was so weak when the cast was removed that the doctor recommended violin lessons to restore the muscles. As a result, a great musical talent was discovered!)

6. Strumming the autoharp or guitar aids in the flexibility and coordination of the fingers and in wrist flexion and extension.

7. Vertical chimes can help to develop muscles that control grasp and release of arms and raising and lowering of arms.

8. The organ has the same advantages as the piano. In addition, because of its sustained tones, it is useful for someone who is missing fingers. Special fingering involving changing of fingers on one key can be worked out, and playing will be smooth and pleasant.

9. Woodwind and brass instruments may aid in breath control and in the movements of the lips and in swallowing.

Miscellaneous Activities for Motor-Impaired Children

All of the adaptations and suggestions indicate how motor-impaired children can participate together with other children in movement activities and in learning to play rhythm and other musical instruments. Many other music activities present no problems, but if the child can't join in all of them, you can easily simplify or adapt some of them slightly, or add or emphasize others.

When the class is dramatizing music, a child confined to a wheelchair can express the music using gestures and facial expressions. Drawing can be another excellent creative outlet to express the music, as can attaching different colored cellophane paper to flashlights and flashing the lights onto a screen to form designs according to the mood, tempo, and form of the musical composition. The children can have poetry and story readings and decide which rhythm instruments are best as background accompaniments.

In musical stage productions, the motor-impaired children can participate by singing in the chorus, providing sound effects, or playing rhythm or melody instruments. They can frequently play solo or lead roles with no lessening of the validity and dramatic effect of the performance.

You can also select, simplify, or adapt for the motor-impaired activities you do with the class when developing the sense of pitch and music reading abilities. For example, an excellent way to help to develop the sense of pitch is to have the children respond with their whole bodies, reaching skyward for high-pitched tones, crouching or bending low for low-pitched tones. Where whole body movements are limited because of physical disabilities, accommodations can be made as follows:

1. Explain to the class that ballplayers have to practice in order to play well, and that it is necessary for them to practice to hear music well. In this game, they will practice "catching" musical "high and low balls." Play a low tone on the melody bells and have the pupils without impairments reach down to the floor and clasp their hands to catch the low ball. Play a high tone and they jump high to catch a "fly" ball. Those children who are confined to wheelchairs can play this game reaching high and low with their arms, or raising and lowering their heads. Other similar imaginative games can be played requiring the children to raise and lower their arms with rising and falling pitch.

2. In a game to practice note reading, have two teams. Every child gets a drawing of a note. There are two drawings of each note for each team. At the signal, each one of the children has to find and stand next to the child on his own team who is holding the same note picture. The first team to have all pairs matched wins. The children who have physical disabilities can participate in this game; they can remain in their seats or wheelchairs and their partners can come to sit next to them.

3. As the rest of the class may be stamping, walking, or dancing to the rhythms of different children's names, the same activity can be done with other movements—tapping the desk, snapping fingers, etc.—to enable the children with physical impairments to participate easily.

4. As the rest of the children play "Freeze" dancing to recordings of music with varying tempos and moods and stopping in posi-

tion when the record is stopped, the motor-impaired children can move their heads or legs, or whatever body parts they can as they remain at their desks, and freeze in position as the music stops.

5. If the children are imitating trains, forming straight lines with each one holding the elbows of the child in front of him and shuffling slowly and then faster and faster, those in the class who cannot do this activity because of physical disabilities can accompany the action by playing maracas, sandpaper blocks or whisties in time to the movements. This will provide excellent sound effects in imitation of the sound of a train.

6. In an exercise to develop rhythm notation reading, several children can step to quarter notes while others walk half (or eighth) notes. They exchange movements when you call "Change." Children with physical disabilities who cannot perform these movements can be the conductors who call out the changes.

The essential precept is that music is for everyone no matter how limited movement may be, no matter what the handicap is—mental, visual, aural, or motor.

". . . Some playing a steady beat, some singing, some reading complex rhythmic or melodic notation, one or two playing autoharp and some playing melody or resonator bells, all of the children can be working together"[12] according to their own intellectual and physical capabilities to perform and to create music.

SUMMARY

More and more motor-impaired children can be found in regular schools and mainstreamed classes. The impairments include loss of limbs or confinement to wheelchairs. To the goals of encouraging communication, enhancing self-image, developing relationships and releasing tensions, there is added the need to strengthen or develop specific muscles or the ability to coordinate movements.

Through the use of prosthetic devices, many such children are able to participate in music activities, all of which should be approved by appropriate medical professionals.

Movement activities include exercises done to music to strengthen the neck, arms or leg muscles, improve balance, crossing of midline, and the like. The musical instruments are selected either because the child's impairment limits his abilities and choices or else because the technique used in playing a specific instrument can serve as exercise to improve functioning. A variety of adaptations (e.g., special beaters, picks, gloves) enable a motor-impaired child to perform a specific instrument. Sometimes, different methods of playing an instrument, such as two children cooperating to play a pair of cymbals or striking chimes with elbows and chin, can be used.

A number of songs with gestures are valuable in providing exercise for hands and fingers, and singing can also aid in developing breath control. In addition, many regular classroom music activities can easily be adapted to include motor-impaired children.

NOTES

[1]Frank R. Wilson, M.D. "Keynote Address, Fourth International Symposium; Music; Rehabilitation and Human Well-Being," August 5, 1985.

[2]"Who Are the De Bolts and Where Did They Get Nineteen Kids?" Public Television, Channel 13. March 18, 1985.

[3]Clark Eddy. "No Fingers to Play a Horn," *Music in Special Education.* Washington, D.C.: Music Educators National Conference, 1972, pp. 45–6.

[4]John Benigno. "Settlement Music School Advances Music for the Handicapped." *Music Educators Journal,* 71, No. 6 (February, 1985), pp. 22–5.

[5]Lucretia Rogers. "Music Therapy in a State Hospital for Crippled Children," in *Music in Therapy*, Thayer Gaston, editor. New York: Macmillan Publishing Company, Inc., 1968, p. 157.

[6]Myra Staum, "Music and Rhythmic Stimuli in the Rehabilitation of Neuromusculoskeletal Gait Disorder." (Unpublished doctoral dissertation, Florida State University, 1981.) *Dissertation Abstracts,* 42A, No. 6, 2553A.

[7]Juliette Alvin. *Music in the Education of the Handicapped Child,* second edition. London: Oxford University Press, 1976, p. 115.

[8]For some of these and additional activities see Donald Michel, *Music Therapy: An Introduction to Therapy and Special Education Through Music.* Springfield, Illinois: Charles C. Thomas, 1976, p. 40; Rogers, "Music Therapy in a State Hospital"; Alvin, *Music for the Handicapped Child,* pp. 137–8.

[9]For further information and detailed drawings and/or descriptions of these original, special instruments, see *They Can Make Music,* by Philip Bailey (London: Oxford University Press, 1973) and *Music Therapy in Special Education* by Paul Nordoff and Clive Robbins (New York: John Day Company, 1971).

[10]Raymond Lewenthal, editor. *Piano Music for One Hand.* New York: G. Schirmer Inc., 1972.

[11]*Guide to the Selection of Musical Instruments with Respect to Physical Ability and Disability.* (Philadelphia, Pennsylvania: Moss Rehabilitation Hospital Settlement Music School Music Program, 1982.)

[12]Ruth Zinar. *Music in Your Classroom.* West Nyack, New York: Parker Publishing Company, Inc., 1983.

C H A P T E R ✖ 8

MUSIC FOR THE
VISUALLY IMPAIRED CHILD

The term "visually impaired" includes both the partially seeing and the blind. An individual is considered to be legally blind if he sees $\frac{20}{200}$ or less with the better eye after correction, or if he has a visual field restricted to less than twenty degrees in the widest diameter. ($\frac{20}{200}$ vision means that one must be twenty feet away to see what a normally sighted person can see at two hundred feet.) Although about six-and-a-half million people in the United States have severely impaired vision and cannot see well even with lenses, most legally blind people do have some usable vision, being able to distinguish light and shadow, see hand movements, or count fingers. Only about twenty percent of the visually impaired are totally blind.

Blindness—which can be congenital or the result of an accident or disease—does not just mean absence of sight. It "changes and utterly reorganizes the entire mental life of the individual."[1] What is the world of a blind child like? Imagine no depth perception, no space, and no form. Verbal descriptions of sights and of visual beauty, space, or color are meaningless. A blind person may repeat descriptions of an object and then be unable to recognize it when he senses it by touch.

Hearing is the most active of all the senses. Many congenitally blind children not only are able to differentiate and recognize voices and other sounds, but also have perfect pitch[2] and by the time they are preschoolers, can remember rhymes and melodies. However, they cannot easily tell from what direction a sound is coming and must learn how to do this and to develop an understanding of the relationship between the sound and the object producing it.

Most of our knowledge of the world comes from our vision, but the congenitally blind baby lacks this stimulation and so turns to his own body. Numerous involuntary mannerisms (sometimes thought of as arising from frustration) can result. Called "blindisms," these include rocking the head and putting fingers into the eyes, ears, nose, and mouth, or manipulating them.

The congenitally blind don't know what it is to see and so don't know what it is they are missing. They would be able to adjust more readily if given the opportunity to develop socially and aesthetically. Actually, they are potentially the same as sighted children but "emotional disturbances result from the social situations that blindness creates and not from the sensory privation itself."[3] Parents of the visually impaired, for example, are frequently over-protective and the child may not be permitted to participate in games with other children. As a result, he can become afraid to move and be awkward or stiff. Little children hit out when they are angry, but the blind child who does that may injure himself, not knowing what or where he may strike. This, and the fact that he doesn't know what is coming towards him, can lead to an accumulation of tension and a tendency toward body inaction.

Sometimes, blind children seem to have more musical talent than sighted children, but this is not so. Musical talent among the blind and partially seeing is the same as for others, but the visually impaired child's handicap results in his developing his hearing ability to a much greater extent. In addition, "music may be more effective and reach him more directly" because when he listens to it, he has no visual images and his response is directed to the sound.[4]

There are a number of practical values for having music activities for the visually impaired. This is partly because their tendency towards lack of voluntary movement can be counteracted by the rhythms of music and music activities. Free rhythmic movement to music can add to bodily freedom and security as well as to grace in walking. Muscle tensions of face, throat, and diaphragm can be relaxed by singing, and songs describing step-by-step procedures in dressing, washing, and social skills can help to teach these.

Blindfolded seeing subjects have been able to learn braille more easily when background music was provided[5] and it is possible that this can also apply to the blind. A two-year study of the use of music therapy showed it to be a "helpful and significant part" of the rehabilitation of up to seventy-seven percent of the subjects.[6]

In addition, music is an area of the curriculum in which the visually impaired can easily participate on the same basis as other children. Visual impairment does not at all affect the muscle abilities needed to play musical instruments and the child's self-image can be enhanced by learning to play. By combining touch, movement, and hearing, music can be of "therapeutic significance for the blind because they are exposed constantly to frustrations that demand emotional release."[7]

Indeed, music has been such a "natural" choice for the blind that there was, in the past, a tendency for some to assume that it should be part of their vocational education. At one time, for example, piano tuning was among the occupations for which they were trained, and in India, it was taken for granted that blind children who would not, as adults, be supported by their families, would probably become basket weavers, beggars, or musicians. Today, many fields of endeavor exist for the visually impaired who study medicine, psychiatry, mathematics, chemistry, law, music, nutrition, etc. Of course, music can be a vocational choice for the blind (Stevie Wonder, Alec Templeton, and Ray Charles are numbered among blind musicians) and many have excelled as performers, especially as "pop" musicians.

More visually impaired children are in public schools than in special schools for the blind. (In New York City, about eighty percent of blind children are in regular schools.[8]) The schools and institutions for the blind used to place more emphasis on music than many mainstreamed public schools do now. It is unfortunate that music is frequently neglected by the mainstreamed public schools because it has the same emotional and intellectual values for the blind and partially seeing that it has for all children. That is why the aesthetic education of the visually impaired must be based upon and must stress the senses he can best use: taste, sound, touch, and smell. It is not necessary for this type of child to see in order to sense beauty in the world—and music obviously plays an important role in this regard. It is "the one art in which the blind are proficient . . . the only art that cannot possibly be subjugated to visual values and visual meanings." It is the one art "so subjective that it is forever put beyond the reach of visual spoliation. . . ."[9]

MUSIC ACTIVITIES

A major goal in the education of the blind and partially seeing is to make them as independent as possible, and there are a number of things which can be done to help achieve this. Sometimes the child senses that his parents worry about his getting hurt, so it is important to make him feel as much at ease in the classroom as possible. To begin with, there is no reason not to be frank about the impairment nor should you be hesitant or self-conscious about using words such as "look" or "see" when you speak to the class.

When the visually impaired child first becomes part of the class, take him on a tour of the room so that he will become familiar with locations of doors, windows, desks, chairs, etc. You could have a clock ticking to assist him in orienting himself, and as soon as possible, let him find his own way around. The youngster needs to learn to become organized, and if ever there was a need for having "a place for everything and everything in its place," it is now. In addition, let the child know if you enter or leave the room or if the position of anything is changed.

It is a good idea to assign either a sighted or partially sighted child as a music partner to help the blind child and also to aid in socialization.

Avoid being over-permissive. Praise the child whenever it is warranted but only for real achievement—not because he has achieved "even tho' " he is blind. As for all other children, teach to his strengths. Therefore, from early infancy and during preschool years, simply shaped, unbreakable toys with sounds—rattles, plastic or rubber balls containing jingling bells, etc.—should be provided, as well as simple objects that can be explored by touch and easily understood (for example, unbreakable bottles and jars, rubber boots, pieces of leather, and cloth of different textures). Playing a musical rattle and letting the child reach out for it helps to develop the ability to find direction of a sound.

Remember to seat the visually impaired where they can hear you well and give instructions orally. Because reading braille is slower than reading regular text (one hundred eighty to two hundred words per minute as compared to five hundred to eight hundred words per minute),[10] assign readings to the blind child ahead of time. Blind children can engage in all kinds of sports including skiing, skating, swimming, wrestling, and bowling.[11] Certainly, with their more highly developed senses of touch and hearing, the regular classroom music curriculum should present few problems and it can be an area in which, with some adaptations of activities and materials, the visually impaired children can excel.

Movement Activities

The visually impaired need many varied activities to develop free-dom of movement. A cleared, uncluttered space should be provided to allow for such activities as walking, dancing, and music dramatizations. All the many natural basic movements in which other children engage can be used and, in addition, relaxation techniques to sedative music should be included. Because blind children cannot see how movements are done, you or a classmate can physically help them to do movements until they learn how. This can be done, for example, by pairing the blind child with one who can see, then with gentle touches or pressures of the hand and quietly spoken cues, the classmate can guide the visually impaired youngster through a dance or movement activity.

Singing Activities

Basically, you can use the same approaches in teaching singing to the visually impaired as you use for normal children. In addition, for the partially seeing, you can prepare enlarged charts and handout sheets and you can use a typewriter with extra-large type for making copies of the words. If any of the partially seeing are in the school choir, place them where they can best see the conductor. You can also make tapes of the songs the class is learning for the visually impaired children to listen to at home in order for them to become more familiar with the words.

Listening Activities

Listening to music and attendance at concerts are excellent activities for the visually impaired. Either you or another person can sit next to the blind child and describe what is happening on stage or at a concert. When the class is learning about instruments of the orchestra or band, the ideal situation would be to have "live" instruments for the blind to touch so that they can learn their shapes and the different "feel" of a brass, string, woodwind, or percussion instrument. This can assist them in associating the tone quality with the source of the sound.

Because the blind need training in telling the direction of sound, it would be helpful to have activities and games in which you play an instrument as you stand in various parts of the room, or you can move around the room while the class tries to guess the direction from which the sound is coming.

Playing Instruments

Participation in rhythm band is no problem; blind children can learn their parts "by ear," and the partially seeing through observation. Hitting instruments, such as drums, can help them release tensions.

To learn other instruments, several approaches are possible. For simple classroom instruments (flutophone, tonette, melody flute, recorder, resonator bells) the most appropriate methods in the average mainstreamed classroom situation would be for you to teach the blind child to play by using his sense of touch and hearing. For this, you can incorporate these steps:

1. Appoint a seeing "buddy," that is, a youngster who has shown better than average performance ability and sense of responsibility. As you give verbal instructions and demonstrate new fingering, have the buddy help the blind child put his or her fingers over the correct holes for wind instruments or move to the correct bars of resonator or song bells.

2. Play new tones or melodies a number of times until the sound is memorized.

3. Have the children practice the fingering or hand movements before they attempt to play.

4. Prepare a special cassette tape for blind children to take home or to listen to in class so that they can be helped to learn "by ear" and aural memory.

5. For the partially seeing, prepare enlarged music charts. The aural memory of partially seeing children is usually not as well-trained as that of the blind pupil, and it is necessary for them to be able to refer to music.

Blind children frequently want to learn to play the piano or an instrument of the band or orchestra. The simplest for them are the valved wind instruments (e.g., trumpet, cornet) that can be fingered with one hand while the music is read by touching a braille music score with the other. Also very suitable are percussion or wind instruments such as the clarinet or flute for which the hands are held in the same position for all notes. However, many blind students and musicians have, in spite of all difficulties, learned to play piano, organ, guitar and violin.

For a blind person to learn to play these instruments, skill in reading braille music notation is needed. This requires instruction by a teacher knowledgeable in reading braille notation, an ability usually taking about a month for a musician to learn. Two of the available manuals for teaching braille music notation are *The Primer of Braille Music*, which can be obtained from the Library of Congress, and *How to Read Braille Music* by Betty Krolick (Champaign, Illinois: Stipes Publishing Company).

Printed music can, at a glance, show musical form and contour (whether the notes are going up or down, whether they move stepwise or "skip"). This is not possible in braille music because only one note at a time can be read and the symbols (like those of literary braille but with different meanings and based on a different system) are written horizontally. Various methods of writing musical braille existed until 1929 when, at the International Conference on Braille Music, progress was made towards establishing some kind of uniformity.[12] Later years saw further simplification, but reading any one note still takes understanding of many separate symbols for the name of the note, the clef, the rhythm duration, whether the note is sharp or flat, etc.

Before a child learns braille notation, he should know literary braille, and before literary braille is taught, work should be done in motor and neural development. If braille notation is to be taught, music lessons are started as rote learning with concurrent instruction in literary braille, music theory, and music listening as well as in playing games to lengthen the aural memory. At New York State School for the Blind, the practice was to have the children start to learn braille music notation in the fourth grade and to have two private music lessons a week.[13]

Reading braille music notation for keyboard music presents special problems. It is impossible to read and play with both hands at one time. The pupil must read one section of music with one hand while the other hand plays its part and then the procedure must be reversed, each small section for each hand being memorized before the two hands play together. Scanning the music visually for its general form or immediately seeing relationships between the two hands is not possible. Chords, written vertically for regular music to show that the tones are played simultaneously, are written in braille music one note at a time with the bottom note indicated first. As a result, "The Moonlight Sonata" takes up more than forty pages of braille music.[14]

Because of these intricacies of braille notation, rote teaching of simple classroom instruments remains the most practical path to take for the classroom and elementary school music teacher. In addition to rote teaching, enlarged music notation should be provided for the partially seeing. In this way, from the very start, their developed senses of touch and hearing will enable the visually impaired to learn easily to play classroom instruments and to participate with other children in most classroom music ensembles.

MUSIC MATERIALS

Basically, music activities and abilities are the same for the visually impaired as for sighted children. Certain additional materials, some with adaptations, are needed that are helpful. Here are some things you can add to the music class:

1. For the partially seeing, make large letters and place them on autoharp bars, melody bells, resonator bells, and piano keys.

2. For the blind, put braille indications on these instruments.

3. Make enlarged charts with the words and music of songs and instrumental pieces and type handout sheets of words of songs using a typewriter with extra-large size type. These are an absolute necessity for the partially sighted.

4. Tie five pieces of heavy cord or wool of contrasting color across a felt board to form a staff. The partially seeing child can readily see this representation and the blind child will be able to touch the cords to feel what a staff is like. The colors easiest for a partially sighted child to see are white cord against a black background.

5. Paste Velcro tabs on the backs of checkers or discs and have these represent notes. The Velcro will easily adhere to your felt board staff and the blind child can, through touching the discs, gain some understanding of the relationships of notes "going up and down," and "skipping" and "walking." The discs can be arranged to form chords to show how simultaneous sounds are represented.

6. Many musical symbols are beautiful in design and aesthetically pleasing. You can make quarter note rests, G clefs, eighth notes,

etc., from pipe cleaners, cut-out pieces of foam rubber, carpet padding, sandpaper, sponges, felt, velvet, brocade, or Velcro. In this way, the blind child will be able to feel them and apprehend their shapes.

7. Special cassette players are available with raised letters, enlarged letters, or colored buttons for the partially seeing or with braille symbols for the blind.

8. The tape recorder is an essential tool for the visually impaired child. Prerecorded accompaniments and practice reminders, songs, and pieces the class is learning can all be taped for extra listening at home or school.

9. Braille music transcriptions are available from the Library of Congress. (These are further described in this chapter's section on resources for the blind.)

10. A "Varispeech" machine is a variable speed tape recorder that can play back at one-half to two and a half times the speed of the original without changing the original pitch and tonal qualities. This is an excellent aid for the visually impaired who can listen to recordings of books, music, or articles at the rate of speed most comfortable for them. And when practicing, the blind student can listen to a slow-playing of a composition as he reads braille music notation, studying and memorizing details of the work.

11. The "Optacon" is not at all related to braille notation. The reader uses a small hand "scanner" to touch the printed page and the print or regular music notation is transformed into a visual display of dots on a small screen (similar to a television screen) and also into tactile stimuli formed by vibrating rods and felt by the index finger of the free hand. The receiver looks much like a small tape recorder, and as the blind person touches it, he feels "tingles" in the shape of the letter or symbol being "scanned"; he "can feel with fingers what the sighted person sees with his eyes."[15]

An Optacon is frequently available for a blind pupil's use from the Commissioner for the Blind (or other appropriate official) in each state. The instrument has the advantage of enabling the blind child to understand what printed music "looks like." There is also no delay in having material transcribed into braille.

12. The Kurzweil Reader transforms printed text into spoken words. This is a very expensive piece of equipment. Sometimes avail-

able at large library centers, it can enable the blind student to hear books about music.

13. The words of some volumes of elementary song book series are available in braille. These have included Silver Burdette's *Making Music Your Own*, the Birchard Music Series, and Ginn and Company's *Singing Every Day*.

MUSIC RESOURCES FOR THE VISUALLY IMPAIRED

1. National Library Services for the Blind and Physically Handicapped of the Library of Congress, Washington, D.C.: Materials include braille scores for piano, voice, choral music, and organ; instructional cassette recordings; large print music scores and books about music; disc recordings of books on music history, theory, analysis, appreciation and biography as well as recordings giving instruction in piano, string instruments, vocal music, guitar, dulcimer, woodwinds, and brass and percussion instruments. In addition, blind and partially seeing students may borrow "The Recorded Aid for Braille Music," a kit including braille, large print and instructional tape recordings for a number of instruments. The music has been "recorded in three different styles: a. reduced tempo with accompaniment, b. recommended tempo without accompaniment, and c. recommended tempo with accompaniment."[16] Thus, the student can work slowly, note by note, as he reads the braille notation or else he can hear the work in parts or in its entirety as it is played in a musical, competent performance.

All of the above are available to the blind without charge, and catalogues can be obtained from the Library of Congress. To be eligible for these services, the visually impaired person must not be able to see well enough to read conventional printing, and verification from a qualified professional is needed.

2. American Printing House for the Blind (P.O. Box 6085, Louisville, Kentucky 40206): Distributes music stands adjustable for distance and publishes graded music song books in extra-large print. Also available are music boards with adhering notes and a catalog of braille music.

3. Paganiniana Publishers, Inc. (P.O. Box 27, Neptune, New Jersey 07753): Prints large note editions of violin sonatas, Bach cello suites, and other such works.

4. The National Society for the Prevention of Blindness (16 East 40th Street, New York, N.Y. 10016): Publishes "A suggested guide to piano literature for the partially seeing" which lists large note solos and collections together with the addresses of publishers from whom they can be obtained.

5. The Louis Braille Foundation for Blind Musicians, Inc. (215 Park Avenue, New York, N.Y. 10003): Transcribes and copyrights works of blind musicians, provides musical instruments for blind music students, and sponsors concerts, providing publicity and promotion for blind performing musicians.

6. The Metropolitan Opera Company (Lincoln Center Special Services, Metropolitan Opera Guild, 1865 Broadway, New York, N.Y. 10023): Provides libretti in braille for blind people in its audience. They also have program notes on cassettes. These summarize the opera and describe the scenery, costumes, and staging, as well as provide information about the composer and background of the opera. Some score desk seats are reserved for the visually impaired; these seats have no view of the stage but the acoustics are excellent and there is a minimal charge for tickets. Backstage tours that include tactile exhibits are provided, and the blind are encouraged to bring seeing-eye dogs or a sighted companion.

7. Recordings for the Blind (with studios in New York City and headquarters at 20 Roszel Road, Princeton, New Jersey 08540): Makes tape recordings and cassettes of textbooks for students. There is no charge for this, and the student is required to provide two copies of the desired text. Of course, books about music are among those taped.

8. National Braille Press, Inc. (83 Stephen Street, Boston): Has volunteers who transcribe music notation into braille.

SUMMARY

Music is the one art in which the blind can excel. As a result of their disability, blind people must depend on their senses of hearing and touch—both essential in music performance—and some have developed exceptional music memories. They are not necessarily more musically talented than the general population, but music is an area in which they can easily participate.

Singing presents no problems for them nor do playing rhythm instruments or listening to music. Tensions resulting from visual impairment can be counteracted by many movement activities and relaxation to music. Braille music notation enables the dedicated and talented to learn instruments of band and orchestra.

Music materials are available from various resources or can be created by the teacher. Felt boards with cord staff lines, enlarged song texts, and musical symbols made of foam rubber, carpet padding, sponges, and pipe cleaners, or enlarged chord indications on autoharp are examples of simple teacher-made materials. Recent developments have made sophisticated instruments such as the Opticon, Vari-Speech tape recorder, and Kurzweil reader available to the blind student. The Library of Congress and the American Printing House for the Blind are among a number of resources that offer special services and materials to visually impaired musicians and music students.

Learning to play a musical instrument with braille music notation requires special instruction. Although reading piano music with braille music notation is quite difficult, this has been accomplished.

Classroom instruments, such as melody flute, can be learned by rote. Touch, hearing, enlarged music or braille notation, and a little extra help from a music "buddy" can enable the visually impaired to participate fully and successfully.

NOTES

[1]Thomas D. Cutsforth. *The Blind in School and Society, new edition.* New York: American Foundation for the Blind, 1972, p. 2.

[2]Ibid., p. 9.

[3]Ibid., p. 122.

[4]Juliette Alvin. *Music for the Handicapped Child*, Second edition. London: Oxford University Press, 1976, p. 130.

[5]Doradeen Perry. "A Study of the Effects of Music on the Learning of Braille by Seeing Subjects," in "Abstracts." *Journal of Music Therapy*, 2, No. 2 (June, 1965), p. 41.

[6]Robert K. Unefker, "Music Therapy in the Rehabilitation of the Adult Blind," in "Abstracts." *Journal of Music Therapy*, 2, No. 2 (Summer, 1965), p. 44.

[7]Sister Josepha, O.S.F. "Music Therapy for the Physically Disabled," in *Music in Therapy*, E. Thayer Gaston, editor. New York: MacMillan Publishing Company, Inc., 1968, p. 111.

[8]Fred Kersten. "Human Well-Being of Visually Impaired Students through Accommodation in Music Classes for the Sighted." Fourth International Symposium: "Music: Rehabilitation and Human Well-Being."

[9]*The Blind in School and Society*, p. 188.

[10]"Human Well-Being of Visually Impaired Students."

[11]Muriel K. Mooney. "Blind Children Need Training, Not Sympathy," in *Music in Special Education*. Washington, D.C.: Music Educators National Conference, 1972, p. 40.

[12]*Revised International Manual of Braille Music Notation, 1956*, American Edition, H.V. Spanner, compiler. Louisville, Kentucky: American Printing House for the Blind, 1961.

[13]Evelyn Kirkland. "Music for Blind Children." *Music Journal*, 30, No. 9 (November, 1972), p. 19.

[14]"Blind Children Need Training," p. 42.

[15]Sandra Levinson. "The Optacon," Fourth International Symposium; "Music; Rehabilitation and Human Well-Being," August 8, 1985.

[16]"Human Well-Being of Visually Impaired Students."

CHAPTER ✖ 9

MUSIC AS AN AID
IN SPEECH REMEDIATION

Speech is needed as a form of communication and as an aid to self-expression. Children who can't make themselves understood have resultant difficulty in communicating and often develop feelings of isolation and frustration. This, in turn, can lead to a hostile attitude toward school, adults, and peers. That is why a serious communication disorder ("any difficulty in producing sounds, words, or sentences"[1]) can affect a child's whole life and his relationships with others.

Deficiencies in speech are among the most common of all impairments, with more children receiving some sort of special help for this than for any other reason. About thirty-five percent of all those pupils who receive some sort of special education do so because of problems with speech[2] and they make up an estimated three percent (some two million)[3] to five percent[4] of the total school population.

Speech involves separate sensory mechanisms, cognitive processes, and physical functions. The air flow from the lungs provides energy for speech. The vocal cords convert the air waves into an audible "buzz." The lips, tongue, and teeth (the articulators) then transfer this buzz into the sounds of speech.[5] Any malfunctions in any of these processes can lead to a speech dysfunction.

In normal speech development, "while a child is learning to refine the phonemes [sounds] he should also be learning the meanings of language."[6] For most children, the basic form or structure of their language has been established by kindergarten or first grade, although errors are still common. These are usually corrected by the second or

169

third grade. If speech dysfunctions have not improved by that time, then "speech improvement" is needed if the problems are mild, "speech therapy" if they are severe.

Some of the speech problems that need help are due to organic causes. For example, there may be hearing loss, nodules on the vocal cords, or dental abnormalities. A cleft palate results in incomplete closure of the midline of lips and roof of the mouth, and although it can be surgically repaired, difficulties in articulation may remain. Cerebral palsy is frequently accompanied by lack of coordination of muscular movements of the tongue and lips. Still other speech problems are functional in nature being affected by social and cultural backgrounds that influence the learning process, language, and speech. Poor habits, laziness, emotional problems, retarded development, and poor role models can all play a part in causing speech problems.

Such disorders take a variety of forms including poor articulation, stuttering, delayed speech, lack of speech, and voice dysfunctions such as harshness, nasality, uncontrolled volume, too soft speech, and lack of variety in pitch (a "monotone" voice).

Among retarded children tested in the early 1970's, the majority had poor, substandard speech,[7] with eight percent having severe defects and with the most frequent problems being those related to voice production and delayed development. In the general school population, the most frequent dysfunction is poor articulation. And the most common types of articulation errors are substitutions (e.g., dis, dat, a vewy pwetty wing), omissions ('ey don' wanna, swee' lan' o' li'ty) and substitutions (Pfred, pfound, a pfeather).

Formerly, many children in regular classes who had mild speech problems were referred to a "communications disorders specialist." Now that more and more children with severe handicaps are in the regular classes, they are the ones who receive special professional help. The less serious errors—especially those related to voice volume and poor articulation—can frequently be helped to some extent in the regular classroom. Whether or not a child should be referred for special help is a decision to be made in consultation with a speech therapist. Situations where a child's disorder stems from organic causes, or where his ability to communicate with his peers is affected, obviously need special attention.

In any event, "speech therapy can be complemented by teachers at every grade level and in all subjects."[8] Experience and studies have shown that music can be a most helpful adjunct in speech therapy and improvement.

USING MUSIC TO IMPROVE SPEECH

One of the earliest uses of music in the diagnosis of speech impairments was that of Jean-Marc Gaspard Itard who, in the early nineteenth century, wrote about his work with "the wild boy of Aveyron," a child found wandering alone in the woods, unable to talk and living like an animal. Edouard Séguin (1812–1880) later developed a method of using music to teach speech skills to the retarded, having them sing vowels and then very gradually add consonants, and finally transfer the sounds to speech.

In the early 1900s, there were the use of singing tones on one vowel sound, humming tunes, and breathing and articulation exercises to correct speech deficiencies. Singing was used in efforts to overcome stuttering and to encourage participation of the silent child. In 1916, it was suggested that music be used to elicit attention and to help discrimination of different sounds.[9] Music was seen as a "stepping-stone to speech."

Some recent studies have demonstrated the usefulness of music as an aid in speech improvement. For example, speech therapy centered around music activities used in programs for speech-delayed children led to greater progress than conventional speech therapy.[10] Speech also improved when music activities were used as a reward for appropriate verbal responses. Handicapped children of three to five years of age, delayed in speech, were shown pictures of common objects and "stories" were read to them about each object. The children were then asked to "tell about the story" and a child giving a correct response could select a music activity. More frequent appropriate answers resulted.[11]

Children with aphasia (lack of speech) have benefitted from combined music and speech therapy.[12] Among twenty cleft palate children, those "treated" with stories using test words set to music "significantly improved over other children given conventional speech therapy."[13] Increased ability in developing the "r" and "s" sounds was specially noted.

Where choral reading and songs were used in a language program for one-and-a-half hours a week for eight weeks, there were "exceptional gains" in both reading and language. "Instruction in choral reading may encourage quantitative fluency in speech and . . . instruction in singing may facilitate accuracy and precision of speech."[14]

Music activities can be included among the many multisense exercises and drills used by speech therapists. "A group of techniques which resolves one client's difficulties" cannot always "apply like a pill to another client having the same or similar difficulties."[15] Therefore, a large repertoire of activities, such as the following, from which to choose is important, and the music and classroom teacher, and, if necessary, the speech teacher, can work together to help improve the speech of children with deficiencies:

1. First of all, set an example with clear enunciation. Listen to your own tape-recorded speech to decide whether you can easily be understood or if any improvement is needed.

2. Have the children with poor speech habits or faulty articulation sit near those who speak clearly.

3. Listen to and show an interest in what a child has to say. Don't interrupt; let him finish. In this way, you will be encouraging fluency in speech.

4. If a child is working to correct a speech disorder, praise him for any improvement.

5. When teaching a sound, have the children first listen to it and then "see" it, watching how you make the sound. After this, they can practice saying it and "feeling" it, sensing, for example, the air blowing against fingers or the vibration or lack of vibration of vocal cords.

6. Let the child record his speech and then listen to evaluate it.

7. Where speech deficiencies are a result of lacks in background, poor models, laziness, habits, and such, determine which dysfunctions occur most frequently in your class and develop pleasant, lively, varied multi-sense games and activities to bring about improvements.

8. Encourage the children to answer in full sentences. If the question, for example, is "What would you like to do?" the answer should be "I want to play" or "I'd like to sing" instead of "Play" or "Sing."

9. Consult with the speech therapist who may be working with a child to find out what sounds or speech problems should be stressed in music activities.

Music for Delayed Speech

In delayed speech, the child hears and sees and has adequate articulators, but does not speak as well as he should at his age. Delayed speech is frequently associated with retardation, but in many cases it is motivation to speak that appears to be missing. The child may respond verbally when stimulated, but otherwise speech is inhibited. Sometimes, communication may take the form of gestures, jargon, or grunts, while "for a few, the problem seems to be emotional; they do not want or dare to talk."[16] For many, the delayed speech can be a result of impoverished background, lack of opportunity to learn language, or actual neglect.

Speech therapists have more than one approach to the problem of delayed speech. One of these, the "synthetic," starts with one sound at a time and then goes on to teach syllables, words, sentences, and finally, spontaneous speech. Sometimes the sounds are taught in alphabetical order, sometimes in the order in which they appear in the development of speech from babyhood, and sometimes in the order of frequency with which they are used in every-day speech. The development of "a sound repertoire based on the acoustic structure of the language is often helpful";[17] when sounds such as "ee," "b," "s," "t" can be produced, the child is taught to say the words "bee," "see," "tea," etc. Some therapists have found this method to be of value not only in treating delayed speech but also for aphasia and articulation and auditory discrimination problems.

Rather than using discrete sounds or nonsense syllables, the "analytic" approach stresses communication. It starts with the word as the smallest meaningful unit as efforts are made through many varied experiences to develop the child's understanding of language.

In either approach, numerous multi-sense activities are used. These include babbling along with the child, kinesthetic experiences, and visual analysis using mirrors to see how sounds are made. Other experiences include drawing, choral reading, training in articulation, actually touching portions of the lips and tongue involved in producing a particular sound, imitation games, finger plays, echoing speech fragments, finding one correctly formed word and working from that, pantomime, playing with toys, speaking in unison with others, and auditory training. One technique involves "silent treatment" and may be used in cases where the child refuses to talk; the therapist remains silent until the child finally breaks the silence by saying something. Or the youngster may be encouraged to talk about his feelings and reactions to his environment.

Music, used in conjunction with many of these techniques, can provide motivation and make drills and repetitions of exercises more enjoyable as well as help to draw the child into verbal expression of his thoughts and feelings. Therapy for delayed speech requires a complex, multifaceted approach to which music activities such as the following can contribute:

1. The song "Pop Goes the Weasel" has tempted more than one child to say his first word. It is sung repeatedly until the child is very familiar with it. Then, one time just before the word "Pop," the teacher stops. The suspense becomes too great; the child calls out, "Pop!"

2. You can add music and song when teaching basic vocabulary and/or expanding the child's knowledge of his environment. For example, animal pictures, animal sounds, stories about animals, toy animals, the song "Old McDonald Had a Farm" and St. Saens' *Carnival of Animals* can all be used to awaken interest and encourage a verbal response.

3. You can teach the alphabet using alphabet blocks, having the children copy letters onto the chalkboard, or tracing them in the air in time to music and having them sing the "Alphabet Song."

4. Teach body parts songs together with movement and have the children suggest body parts. Movement to songs about "up" and "down," "left" and "right," and "over" and "under" can help to teach these words, and singing songs about colors and drawing and painting to music can provide additional experiences when the children are learning to name colors. (See Chapter 4, "Music for the Trainable Retarded Child" for examples of body parts, "direction" and "color" songs.)

5. The kazoo is a useful instrument. Let the child "play" a melody by humming into the kazoo and then little by little show him how he can hum without the instrument. Gradually add the words of the song.

6. Play the "Kazoo-Bee" game. The child "buzzes" like a bee using the kazoo and then, "landing" on an object in the room with the kazoo, names the object.

7. Play a recording and let the child express the music through pantomime. Then encourage him to "tell the story" explaining the pantomime.

8. If the child is in the "babbling" stage, have him march around the room to appropriate music, babbling in time to the beat of the drum. Teach the words, "Boom! Boom!" and have him chant that along with the babbling. Little by little, add other words.

9. Play a recording and encourage the child to express verbally how the music makes him feel.

10. Let the child have frequent experiences being with other children as they sing and play music games. The enjoyment and relaxation he can feel plus the new vocabulary being learned through songs can enhance verbal responses.

11. Try to teach songs using the new words the child has learned —especially those taught by the speech therapist.

12. Start with very simple, repetitious songs using few words and gradually have them increase in complexity as the child's language abilities grow.

Music Activities to Develop Auditory Discrimination

Auditory discrimination is very important in learning to speak and in speech improvement. If a child does not hear or distinguish sounds, he will certainly have difficulty in reproducing them. Music activities, such as the following, can be especially helpful in encouraging careful listening:

1. Play a single tone on a toy piano or on melody bells and then have the child try to find the correct key or bar on which to play the same tone. When skill is developed finding the one tone, do the same thing with a two-note and then a three-note pattern.

2. Show the child three bells from the resonator bells set, selecting those that form a simple chord (e.g., C, E, G; G, B, D; or F, A, C). As the children watch, play and name the three tones, ask them which one you played last. Now hide the bells and play them in any order, and have the children try to guess which one you played last. A child who guesses correctly can come to the front of the room and be the one to play the bells next. Repeat this several times. This can also be done using Swiss melody bells.

3. Play a tone on the recorder, melody bells, or song flute and have the children sing the echo. Then do the same thing with two- and three-note patterns and, finally, with short phrases.

4. Show the children a group of familiar classroom instruments, then have them hide their eyes. Play one of them and have the youngsters guess which one you played.

5. Play a variation of the childhood "telephone" game. Call one child to the front of the room and very softly "whisper sing" a brief fragment into his ear. This child then chooses another child to whom to sing and so on, until a number of children have heard the song fragment. Ask the last child to sing what he heard. Then you sing the original tones while the rest of the class decides if the final version was the same or different.

6. Play a very brief melody on melody bells and then repeat it, changing one tone. Have the children raise their hands when they hear your "mistake."

7. Play the game in which you move around the room beating a drum as the children, eyes closed, point to the direction from which they hear the sound.

8. Play "echos." You can make up your own melodic fragments and have the children sing back what they hear. Some examples of suitable melodies are:

Yoo - hoo!   I   see   you   It's   goin' to rain to - day   Good - bye, now

9. Play the "Listen Game." Have the children close their eyes for three minutes and try to hear all the sounds around them. Then have them write out a list of sounds they heard or tell you about them.

10. Play a variation of the same game. Have the children close their eyes and listen while you sing part of a song as softly as possible. Then ask them if they can tell you the words of the song you sang. This game and the one above require full concentration.

Music Activities to Aid in the Correction of Voice Dysfunctions

Voice disorders can be due to organic or functional causes. Physical problems of larynx, oral or nasal cavities, or breathing disorders can be involved. The mouth opening may be too small or the tongue elevated too much at the back of the mouth. Habit and cultural influences can also play a part in creating the dysfunction. Teachers are not always aware that a child has a voice problem or "even if . . . conscious of a child's vocal disturbance . . . does not relate the . . . problem to the speech therapist's work and interest."[18] A noticeable voice deviation should be checked to make sure that there is no underlying medical problem.

MUSIC ACTIVITIES TO COUNTERACT NASALITY

In addition to an organic problem, nasality can result from inactivity of the soft palate. To encourage a more "open" sound, speech therapists have frequently used "blowing" exercises. However, because the method of breathing used for blowing is actually different from that used in speech, humming is considered by some to be more useful. The music activities most valuable as an aid in correcting nasality are humming, playing the kazoo (which is "played" by humming into the instrument), and singing—especially practicing singing the vowel sounds "ah," "ă," "ow," "oh," and "ī." Playing simple classroom wind instruments such as melody bells or flutophone are also useful.

MUSIC ACTIVITIES TO AID IN CORRECTING
VOLUME DISORDERS

A too loud, booming voice can be a disorder, sometimes resulting from overenthusiastic lack of control or from growing up in a home where everyone tries to outshout the rest of the family. Sometimes the child simply hasn't learned what kind of voice is appropriate for various situations. The child who speaks too softly may not realize he isn't being heard, or may do so because of shyness or because at home no one listens to him anyway. Or the problem may be due to incorrect breathing, faulty resonance, or inadequate voice projection.

The following music activities can be of help:

1. Have the children try to sing the same song at different intensity levels to become aware of differences in degrees of loudness.

2. Teach lullabies and sedative songs. When they are familiar with them, tell the children that you will sing a lullabye to them. Then, in a loud voice, start to bellow "Lullabye, and Goodnight," or

"Hush, Little Baby." They will undoubtedly react to the incongruous humor, telling you that you are singing too loud. Explain to them that there are times that a soft voice is more appropriate.

3. Relate degrees of loudness of voice to the concepts of a music "crescendo" ⏜⏜ (gradually becoming louder) and "decrescendo" ⏞⏞ (gradually becoming softer). Have the class make up a chant on any given topic and recite it, gradually increasing and then decreasing in volume as you point to the symbols ⏜⏜ and ⏞⏞.

4. Relate music dynamics symbols to different speech situations:

Whispering to your neighbor:	pp, very soft, "pianissimo."
Speaking to your neighbor:	mp, medium soft, "mezzo piano."
Speaking to the class:	mf, medium loud, "mezzo forte."
Playing outside, shouting:	f, loud, "forte."
Calling someone far away:	ff, very loud, "fortissimo."

Then point to the different symbols and have the children speak or chant a phrase in the appropriate tone of voice.

5. Remove the symbols and just point to the description of one of the speech situations. Have the children chant or speak a phrase in the appropriate voice.

6. Imitate the sounds of trains, starting to say "chug, chug," very softly and gradually increasing, then decreasing volume to represent trains coming closer and going away. This can also be related to the ⏜⏜ ⏞⏞ symbols. You can add rhythm instruments (tambourines, sandpaper blocks, maracas) and whistles to enhance the effect.

7. As you point to the symbols ⏜⏜ ⏞⏞, have the children imitate the wind as they sing "OO_____."

8. Have the children sing "echo" songs. Divide the class in half and have the first group sing one phrase at a time in a normal voice with the other half being the "echo." Then have them change places. Examples of echo songs found in other chapters of this book are "Oh, How Lovely Is the Evening" (Chapter 2), "Goodbye, Old Paint" (Chapter 5), and "Frère Jacques" (Chapter 4). Some additional echo songs are:

OH, BURY ME NOT ON THE LONE PRAIRIE

Cowboy Song

SCOTLAND'S BURNING

English Folk Song

WHEN THE SAINTS GO MARCHING IN

Verse 2: Oh, when the sun (oh, when the sun) refuse to shine (refuse to shine),
Oh, when the sun refuse to shine,
Oh, Lord, I want to be in that number. . . .

9. Have the children whose voices are too soft sing any tone on the syllable "oo" and then gradually increase the intensity level as they raise their hands or arms.

10. Children whose voices are inaudible may have faulty resonance. Having them sing songs, such as the following, imitating chimes or do vocal imitations of drums may help to overcome this:

WESTMINSTER CHIMES

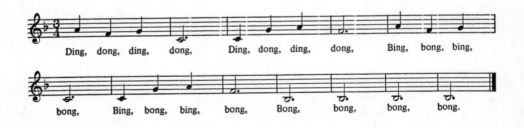

DRUM SONG

11. Encourage the child with poor breathing capacity (a possible cause of inaudibility) to play a wind instrument such as flute or recorder.

12. Gradually increase the phrase lengths of songs to help develop breath control.

13. Encourage the child with an inaudible voice to play the harmonica. This has been found to be valuable in increasing breath capacity.

MUSIC ACTIVITIES TO COUNTERACT MONOTONE SPEECH

Monotone speech can be due to various causes: habit, shortness of breath, abnormal breathing, or physical problems with larynx or nasal cavities. Music activities cannot correct the organic conditions, but where speech therapy is being used, they can help provide additional practice by stressing pitch matching and the concepts of "high" and "low." For example:

1. Have the children imitate fire sirens, raising and lowering arms with the rising and falling pitch.

2. Have the pupil sing any tone at all and then imitate him. Now you sing the next highest tone and have him try to imitate you as he raises both arms. When he can successfully do this, transfer the variation in pitch to a brief, two-syllable word or chant. Gradually increase the vocal range one note at a time, first singing and then chanting and speaking.

3. Have the children dramatize stories that would require them to speak in different tones of voice (e.g., "Goldilocks and the Three Bears," "Billy Goats Gruff"). You can set some of the speeches to "music":

THE THREE BEARS

Father Bear: Some - one's been sit - ting in my chair!

Mother Bear: Some - one's been sit - ting in my chair!

Baby Bear: Some - one's been sit - ting in my chair!   *etc.*

4. Use many activities combining voice and body, such as having the children sing an ascending scale as they reach higher and higher. See-saw chants also emphasize the ups and downs of pitch.

5. Have the children sing swinging songs as they accompany their singing with appropriate body movements:

SWINGING SONG

Music Activities to Aid in the Correction of Misarticulation

Misarticulation accounts for two-thirds[19] to three-quarters[20] of speech disorders and if not corrected becomes more noticeable as the child matures. What is charming when a three-year-old says, "I twied to wun" is unfortunate at ten years of age. Frequently, misarticulation errors are functional and result from carelessness, laziness, poor role models, dialect, or cultural background. Sometimes they are due to the lack of muscle tone and control of the tongue and jaw present in cerebral palsy, or due to a cleft palate, muscular dystrophy, hearing loss, lack of strength or speed of movements of lips or tongue, or even to the temporary loss of a tooth.

Frequently, a specific disability will be treated by speech therapists with similar techniques regardless of cause.[21] Some special techniques are needed, for example, for the child with cerebral palsy, but "much of his therapy regime parallels treatment for cases who do not have cerebral palsy" and the child's "predominant needs may resemble those of functional cases who misarticulate for non-organic reasons."[22]

Children who have articulation problems as a result of physical disabilities such as cerebral palsy or cleft palate will have the special help of speech therapists. In addition, they should have the opportunity to express themselves musically and to participate in music activities without concern for framing words. This can be accomplished through appropriate music games, listening to music, and playing instruments that require minimum lip movement (e.g., harmonica and flutophone).

In addition, assuming that these children are working with a speech therapist, that all needed medical care is provided, and that the music activities are chosen in consultation with the speech therapist, specific sounds can be practiced using a number of songs, chants, and pleasant music activities.

And the same songs and activities can be used with children with less severe impairments as well as for those who merely have to learn how to frame a sound accurately. "Much of the standard school curriculum may be adapted to fit the speech needs of pupils either with or without cerebral palsy"[23] and music can be of special value. If children "have an opportunity to hear and sing difficult sound combinations over and over again in their favorite songs and singing games, they . . . begin to recognize them and then may try to reproduce the intriguing sounds."[24]

ACTIVITIES FOR GENERAL IMPROVEMENT OF ARTICULATION

1. Have the children sing any song and then repeat it several times, each time getting softer and softer until they can barely be heard. As they sing more softly, their articulators will tend to become more active.

2. Now have them "mouth" the song in exaggerated fashion, "lipping" the words without making any sound at all. This is a good exercise for mobility of lips and tongue.

3. Play a guessing game. Have one of the children come to the front of the room and move his mouth as if he is singing a song, "lipping" the words while the rest of the class tries to guess the song.

4. Have the children clap all the syllables of a song so that they become conscious of the number of syllables that must be sounded. This can help to overcome omissions.

5. Have the children sing a song in "slow motion" to give them the chance to become aware of all the movements of the mouth that are needed to form the words.

ACTIVITIES TO CORRECT SPECIFIC ARTICULATION ERRORS

Activities to correct specific articulation errors involve singing or chanting sentences, phrases, or little songs that concentrate on specific sounds. Remember that for each sound the children should *hear* you say it, *watch* your mouth as you say it, *practice* making the sound, and *sense* through touch to find out what is happening to the vocal cords, lips, and breath.

"P" Games and Songs

1. Have the class sing "Pop Goes the Weasel" exaggerating the "p" sounds as they are reached.

2. Give each of the children a thin strip of paper to hold up in front of their mouths as they sing a scale on the syllables, "Pah, pah, pah...." The papers should move with each properly produced tone.

3. A good "P" song is the tongue-twister "Peter Piper." The youngsters can use the strips of paper or else hold their hands in front of their mouths to feel the percussive quality of the "pah" sound as they sing, to the tune of "Yankee Doodle":

> Peter Piper picked a peck,
> A peck of pickled peppers,
> How many pecks of picked peppers
> Did Peter Piper pick?

4. Do the same thing as the children sing an "Oom-pah-pah" song:

"OOM PAH PAH"

Oom - pah - pah,   Oom - pah - pah,   Oom - pah - pah,   Oom!   Oom!

5. Have the children imitate motor boats as they chant the following, starting very slowly and gradually increasing the speed as they become skillful at making the sound:

Putt - putt - putt - putt - putt - putt - putt - putt - putt - putt, *etc.*

"B" Games and Songs

1. Have the pupils hold their palms in front of their mouths to feel their breath as they sing "bells" songs such as "Westminster Chimes." (The "Westminster Chimes" song can be found in the section dealing with voice dysfunction earlier in this chapter.)

2. Give each child a piece of tissue paper and have them roll it into a little ball. Now have them sing "My Bonnie Lies Over the Ocean" with their faces held close to the paper and with the "B" sounds exaggerated. The paper will move each time the sound is produced correctly:

MY BONNIE

3. Have several children get down on all fours, each one putting his mouth close to the rolled up piece of paper and trying to move the paper a little bit across the room each time one of the following syllables is sung:

Bah, Bay, Bee, Bo, Boo, Bee, Bo, Boo!

4. Have the children try to sing the "tongue-twister" below based on the "B" sound:

BETTY BARTER

Bet - ty Bar - ter bought a bit, a bit of bet - ter but - ter.

But we found the but - ter bit - ter Bet - ty Bar - ter bought.

MISCELLANEOUS GAMES AND ACTIVITIES FOR ARTICULATION

1. A variation of "Little Tommy Tinker" provides good practice for the "T" sound:

LITTLE TOMMY TINTER

Lit - tle Tom-my Tin - ter sat on a splin - ter, He be - gan to cry, Boo - hoo! Too true! Tee - ny, ti - ny in - no - cent guy.

2. Sing sibilant songs and perform chants using the "S" sound to help to overcome a lisp. For example:

SINGING SUSIE
(To the tune of "Cindy")

See sing - ing Su - sie slide and slip, She skates on slip - p'ry ice,

See sing - ing Su - sie slide and slip as skat - ing seems so nice.

3. The following song emphasizes the "R" sound as it occurs at the beginning and the end of words:

THE MERRY-GO-ROUND

Mer - ry - go - round, go round, go round, round and round the ring, _____
Mer-ry - go - round, go round and round, Try to reach for the pret - ty ring._____

4. A good song for highlighting the correct use of "th" in place of "t" or "d" is "This Land is Your Land." Not only does the word "this" recur in the refrain, but it is an accented, important word in the last measures when the text declares, "*This* land was made for you and me."

5. Work on the consonant sounds being practiced with the speech therapist. Prepare cards with a different sound indicated on each (e.g., "b," "t," "d," "l") and place them in a box or bag. Have a child select one of the cards and then have the class "sing" a familiar song just using the sound selected (i.e., If the child picks "l," the class might sing the melody of "This Old Man" on the syllable "la"; if "b" is picked, the children will sing "bah" throughout).

6. Have a set of alphabet blocks with a different letter on each side. Let a child toss one of the blocks into a blanket and then have the class sing nonsense syllables using the letter seen on top of the block.

Music Activities for Aphasia

Aphasia is the complete lack of speech and it is associated with brain injury or diseases which affect neurological control. The left hemisphere of the brain controls the logical and verbal, the right side, nonverbal functions. Because singing and other musical activities are primarily functions of the right side of the brain, if the left hemisphere is damaged, singing can be regained and sometimes, through singing, speech. The connections among song, music, and speech are demonstrated by the fact that "defects in the music functions appear almost invariably along with incapacities in other psychomotor functions of which the foremost is speech."[25]

Sometimes people who have lost the ability to speak can sing provided that they can still understand language. Melodic Intonation Therapy (MIT), developed in the early 1970s, can help. It is a "compensatory strategy . . . retrieving language in aphasia patients when all other forms of therapy [have] failed."[26] In this method, short phrases and sentences are sung in very simple melodic patterns approximating speech but "exaggerating the intonation, rhythm stress and melodic contours of speech inherent in the undamaged right hemisphere." The melody is performed at a much slower pace than speech and a limited range of tones is used:

Ex.

Hel - lo   What   is your name?   How   *are*   you?   What   do you want?

Gradually, the sentences are increased in length and little by little the song quality is changed to chant and then to speech, as language to express thoughts is encouraged rather than just the echoing of learned phrases. It is rare to have an aphasic child in a class, but some of the methods used in MIT can be helpful and music can also be a valuable transition to speech communication, as a form of emotional expression, and as a means of establishing relationships with others.

To help an aphasic child through music:

1. Use a much slower than average tempo for songs as speech is relearned.

2. Use songs with regular, simple rhythms.

3. Use songs requiring few words.

4. Help the child to remember the words of a song by providing visual "cues" in the form of pictures or diagrams.

5. While singing is an important activity to help in regaining speech, whistling, tone matching, and articulation exercises are also useful.

6. In addition, give the child many opportunities to express feelings through nonverbal means including pantomime, drawing, painting, dancing, and gesturing to music.

Music and Stuttering

Stuttering can have various causes and affects about five percent of the children (mostly males) who have speech problems.[27] If started early in life, it is frequently ignored in the hope that the child will outgrow it, but it can become habitual. Because it can be a result of physical causes or tensions, stuttering may become worse as the child matures. He should therefore be checked to determine whether there are neurological components or emotional pressures. Two basic corrective techniques are used by therapists: one works to correct symptoms and formations of individual sounds and the other to improve fluency.

Because of the strong emotional component involved in stuttering, there are certain things you can do to help the child, as follows:

1. Remember that perfection of speech is rarely possible and many mild "dysfluencies" are normal.
2. Because stammering and stuttering increase when someone is tired or under pressure, try to see that the child is not fatigued or tense.
3. Encourage the child to speak more slowly.
4. Don't interrupt the child's speech or "fill in" words for him.
5. While you should call on the child, don't place him in situations where he would be expected to speak for any length of time.
6. Give the child the opportunity to use speech in "safe" situations: choral speaking, rote experiences, and above all, singing. This will give him the chance to practice and to identify with the other children.

Most stutterers do not stutter when they sing. For this reason, many efforts have been made—from the days of Ancient China and Greece and biblical times to today—to cure stuttering through singing activities. Unfortunately, although many studies show that there is improvement *while singing*, there is no evidence to show that singing can cure stuttering.[28] Some related activities have helped. These include chanting with the use of a metronome (an instrument that keeps time by "ticking" at various selected rates of speed) and doing "Calypso" singing in which the child tells stories by improvising chants. Although singing cannot cure stuttering, it can still provide "benefits from participating vocally in a normal and satisfying manner, from feeling the flow and the momentum of oral production."[29]

This experience of participation and enjoyment together with other children can enhance the child's ability to feel at ease with others and may help to reduce some of the tensions associated with stuttering.

Song means more than a "tune"; the words are as important as the melody in speech remediation. Again and again, music has been proven to be a powerful motivating force in the lives of children. Adding music to speech sounds can make speech therapy for misarticulation and voice dysfunction more fun. Singing words of songs can enhance language, expand the child's vocabulary, and help to correct speech disorders.

SUMMARY

There are more children with impaired speech than with any other disability. Speech therapists deal with the most severe problems, but classroom and music teachers can play a role in supplementing their work and can also help children with less severe problems.

The most frequent problem is that of misarticulation—lisping, mispronouncing specific sounds, and omitting sounds. "Tongue twisters" set to music and some music games can be helpful. Voice dysfunctions such as nasality and volume disorders can also be helped: humming, singing, and playing wind instruments counteract nasality; some volume disorders can be alleviated by songs and games that stress "echos" or practice rhythm chants at various levels of intensity.

The development of pitch awareness through body movement and song are used to create variety in a monotone voice. A harsh voice can imply some physical disorder and should be checked by a physician.

Delayed speech is a frequent problem and can be due to retardation or emotional or environmental causes. Speech therapists frequently use the same methods to treat a specific disability regardless of cause and the multi-sense appeal of music activities can help children communicate.

Aphasia is treated by speech professionals. One approach, Melodic Intonation Therapy, uses brief melodic fragments sung rhythmically as speech is gradually restored. Although people who stutter frequently do not do so when they sing, music and song have no lasting effect on this dysfunction.

Because words and music are united in "song," singing has been shown to be of great value in overcoming speech disorders.

NOTES

[1]Kathleen W. McCartan. *The Communicatively Disordered Child.* Hingham, Massachusetts: Teaching Resources Corporation, 1977, Introduction.

[2]Richard M. Graham and Alice S. Beer. *Teaching Music to the Exceptional Child.* Englewood Cliffs, New Jersey, Prentice-Hall, Inc., 1980, p. 14.

[3]Richard Graham. "Seven Million Plus Need Special Attention. Who Are They?" *Music in Special Education.* Washington, D.C.: Music Educators National Conference, 1972, p. 7.

[4]George O. Egland. *Speech and Language Problems; A Guide for the Classroom Teacher.* Englewood Cliffs, New Jersey, Prentice-Hall, Inc., 1970.

[5]*Learning Difficulties: Oral Language Development.* Louisville, Kentucky: Jefferson County Board of Education, 1976, p. ix.

[6]*Speech and Language Problems*, p. 27.

[7]*Speech for the Retarded Child.* New York City: Bureau of Curriculum Development of the Board of Education, reprinted in 1971, p. 106.

[8]*Speech and Language Problems*, p. 58.

[9]Alan L. Solomon. "Music in Special Education Before 1930; Hearing and Speech Development." *Journal of Research in Music Education*, 28, No. 4 (Winter, 1980), p. 240.

[10]Christine Harding and Keith D. Ballard. "The Effectiveness of Music as a Stimulus and as a Contingency Reward in Promoting the Spontaneous Speech of Three Physically Handicapped Pre-Schoolers." *Journal of Music Therapy*, 19, No. 2 (Summer, 1982), pp. 86–101; Charles D. Seybold, "The Value and Use of Music Activities in the Treatment of Speech Delayed Children." *Journal of Music Therapy*, 8, No. 3 (Fall, 1971), pp. 102–110.

[11]"The Effectiveness of Music as a Stimulus and as a Contingency Reward."

[12]Tricia Krauss and Herbert Galloway. "Melodic Intonation Therapy with Language Delayed Apraxic Children." *Journal of Music Therapy*, 19, No. 2 (Summer, 1982), pp. 102–113.

[13]Donald E. Michel and Nancy Hudgens May. "The Development of Music Therapy Procedures with Speech and Language Dis-

orders." *Journal of Music Therapy*, 11, No. 2 (Summer, 1974), pp. 74–80.

[14]Randall Keith Bassett. "An Investigation of the Effects of Instructional Programs of Choral Reading and Singing on Language Achievement and Oral Language Development of Sixth Grade Students." (Unpublished doctoral dissertation, The University of Tennessee, 1979) DA 40, No. 6, p. 3078.

[15]James Neal Blake. *Speech, Language and Learning Disorders; Education and Therapy.* Springfield, Illinois: Charles C. Thomas Publishers, 1971, p. 41.

[16]"The Value and Use of Music Activities in the Treatment of Speech," p. 102.

[17]*Speech, Language and Learning Disorders*, p. 41.

[18]Ibid., p. 123.

[19]"Seven Million Need Special Attention," p. 7.

[20]*Speech and Language Problems*, p. 98.

[21]*Music in Therapy*, E. Thayer Gaston, editor. New York: Macmillan Publishing Company, Inc., 1968, p. 121.

[22]*Speech and Language Problems*, p. 136.

[23]Ibid., pp. 136–7.

[24]Verna Breinholt and Irene Schoepfle. "Music Experiences for the Child with Speech Limitations." *Music Educators Journal*, 47, No. 1 (September–October, 1960), p. 46.

[25]George A. Giacobbe. "Music Builds Order in Brain Damaged Children." *Music in Special Education*, p. 25.

[26]Melodic Intonation Therapy with Language Delayed Apraxic Children," p. 102.

[27]*Speech and Language Problems*, p. 185.

[28]Herbert F. Galloway, Jr., "Stuttering and the Myth of Therapeutic Singing." *Journal of Music Therapy*, 4, No. 4 (Winter, 1974), pp. 202–7.

[29]Speech and Language Problems, p. 228.

Bibliography

Alvin, Juliette. *Music for the Handicapped Child*, second edition. London: Oxford University Press, 1976.

Bailey, Philip. *They Can Make Music*. London: Oxford University Press, 1973.

Cutsforth, Thomas D. *The Blind in School and Society*, new edition. Louisville, Kentucky: American Printing House for the Blind, 1972.

Dobbs, Jack P.B. *The Slow Learner and Music*. London: Oxford University Press, 1966.

Farnsworth, Paul. *The Social Psychology of Music*, second edition. Iowa State University Press, 1969.

Gaston, Thayer, editor. *Music in Therapy*. New York: Macmillan Publishing Company, Inc., 1968.

Graham, Richard and Alice Beer. *Teaching Music to the Exceptional Child*. Englewood Cliffs: Prentice Hall, Inc., 1980.

Guide to the Selection of Musical Instruments with Respect to Physical Ability and Disability. Philadelphia, Pennsylvania: Moss Rehabilitation Hospital and Settlement Music School, 1982.

Michel, Donald. *Music Therapy: An Introduction to Therapy and Special Education Through Music*. Springfield, Illinois: Charles C. Thomas, 1976.

Music in Special Education. Washington, D.C.: Music Educators National Conference, 1972.

Nordoff, Paul and Clive Robbins. *Music in Special Education*. New York: John Day Company, 1971.

Readings in Trainable Mentally Handicapped. Guilford, Connecticut: Special Learning Corporation, 1980.

Readings: Developing Arts Programs for Handicapped Students, editor, Lola Kearns et al. Philadelphia, Pennsylvania: Arts in Special Education Project of Pennsylvania, [1981].

Revised Manual of Braille Music Notation, H.V. Spanner, compiler. Louisville, Kentucky: American Printing House for the Blind, 1961.

Ross, Alan O. *Learning Disabilities; The Unrealized Potential.* New York: McGraw Hill Book Co., 1977.

Schoen, Max. *The Effects of Music.* Freeport, New York: Books for Libraries Press, 1968.

Journals:

American Journal of Mental Deficiency
American Music Teacher
Journal of Music Therapy
Journal of Research in Music Education
Music Educators Journal
New York State School Music News
Volta

Appendix

RECOMMENDED RESOURCES

Adair, Audrey. *Ready to Use Music Activities Kit.* West Nyack: Parker Publishing Company, Inc., 1985.

Adler, Ruthlee. *Target on Music.* (Includes teacher created songs and activities to achieve specific skills.) Bethesda, Maryland: Christ Church Children's Center, 1984.

Anderson, William M. and Jay E. Lawrence. *Integrating Music Into the Classroom.* (Chapters 7 and 8 deal with the relationship of music to Social Studies and the arts.) Belmont, California: Wadsworth Publishing Company, 1985.

Athey, Margaret and Gwen Hotchkiss. *A Galaxy of Games for the Music Class.* (Simple activities for teaching basic music notation and concepts.) West Nyack: Parker Publishing Company, Inc., 1975.

Birkenshaw, Lois. *Music for Fun, Music for Learning,* second edition. (Early childhood songs for teaching basic life skills and concepts.) Toronto: Holt, Rinehart and Winston of Canada, Ltd., 1977.

Ginglend, David and Winifred Stiles. *Music Activities for the Retarded Child.* New York: Abington Press, 1965.

Krout, Robert. *Teaching Basic Guitar Skills to Special Learners.* St. Louis, Missouri: MMB Music, Inc.

Lewenthal, Raymond, editor. *Piano Music for One Hand.* New York: G. Schirmer, Inc., 1972.

Vernazza, Marcelle. *Music Plus for the Young Child in Special Education.* (A song collection.) Boulder, Colorado: Pruett Publishing Company, 1978.

Wheeler, Lawrence and Lois Raebeck. *Orff and Kodály Adapted for the Elementary School,* third edition. Dubuque, Iowa: Wm. C. Brown, Publishers, 1985.

Zinar, Ruth. *Music in Your Classroom.* (Simple activities for teaching basic concepts and notation and for relating music to classroom curriculum; uses a creative approach.) West Nyack: Parker Publishing Company, Inc., 1983.

Recordings:

*Kimbo Educational Division; P.O. Box 477A, Long Branch, New Jersey 07746.

Adaptive Motor Learning
Dance Therapy Techniques
Finger Play and Hand Exercises
Learning Basic Skills Through Music, Volumes I–IV
Mainstreaming Movement
Songs About Me
Songs for Music Therapy
Special Exercises for Exceptional Children

Orchestrated Music for Special Children (selected compositions with suggestions for their use in achieving specific goals). Hector Records, Waldwick, New Jersey 07463.

Miscellaneous:

Single reed horns can be obtained from: Magna-Music Baton Inc., 10370 Page Industrial Boulevard, St. Louis, Missouri 63132.

A large variety of classroom instruments and catalogues can be obtained from the following:

Sam Ash Music Corporation: 142 Fulton Avenue; Hempstead, New York 11550.

Children's Music Center, Inc. (also has recordings): 5373 W. Pico Boulevard, Los Angeles, California 90019.

Rhythm Band, Inc.: Post Office Box 126, Fort Worth, Texas 76101.

Suzuki: P.O. Box 261030, San Diego, California 92126.

---

*Available recordings change from time to time, so check with the company.

Index